SAM
JONES

GREAT PULPIT MASTERS

SAM JONES

INTRODUCTION BY

BISHOP IVAN LEE HOLT

BAKER BOOK HOUSE
Grand Rapids, Michigan

ISBN: 0-8010-5054-5
Copyright 1950
Fleming H. Revell Company
Reprinted 1973 by Baker Book House Company
by permission of Fleming H. Revell Company

PHOTOLITHOPRINTED BY CUSHING - MALLOY, INC.
ANN ARBOR, MICHIGAN, UNITED STATES OF AMERICA
1973

CONTENTS

A GENIUS OF THE PULPIT

SAM JONES DIED OVER A GENERATION AGO, BUT HIS REPU-
tation as a unique preacher and a master of audiences still
lives. At the funeral service the eloquent Bishop Charles
B. Galloway characterized him thus: "What strange para-
doxes were wrapped up in this masterful man and his bril-
liant career! He was a genius without eccentricity, a great
personality without peculiarities, unique without being
erratic, a wonderful orator without the rules of oratory, a
marvelous preacher with little concern for homiletics."

In his biography of this great preacher his son-in-law,
Dr. Walt Holcomb, tells a number of stories which reveal
much of the heart and personality of Sam Jones. "He liked
people, rich and poor, black and white, saint and sinner,
Protestant and Catholic. In Baltimore some sectarian
brother asked him why he didn't jump on the Catholics.
'When I get through with the Methodists it's bedtime,'
was his tolerant reply." On the night before he died he was
on a Rock Island train en route to Memphis. He saw in the
coach a sick man being taken home by his wife, who
seemed herself almost exhausted. He asked the Pullman
conductor to bring them to the Pullman, and he himself
paid the extra fare. Finding that the man was dying from
tuberculosis and wanted to go home to die, Sam Jones

promised them more money in the morning on arrival at Memphis. Early the next morning, about six o'clock, he died before the train reached Memphis. The money was taken from his clothes by his son-in-law, who had heard the promise, and the sick man was sent home.

On the chautauqua platform he was such a popular lecturer that he always drew great crowds. In the company of such lecturers as W. J. Bryan, Robert M. La Follette and Governor J. Frank Handly it was Sam Jones who did the talking, and they did the listening. His body lay in state in the capitol building in Atlanta, and more than thirty thousand people passed by the casket to pay their respects. In that same city of Atlanta, a year earlier, President Theodore Roosevelt called Sam Jones to the speaker's platform and said to him, "Sam, you have been doing as a private citizen what I have tried to do as a public servant." The vast audience cheered and cheered!

It is doubtful that any preacher in America, within the limit of the same preaching years, ever spoke to so many people or ever moved them to such decisions. There was antagonism to his scathing denunciations of sin and sinners, and he was threatened, or sometimes his property was destroyed and he was attacked physically. His homely wit is illustrated by a story from St. Louis. A committee waited on him after some days of preaching and said, "We brought you here to pitch into sinners and you have pitched into us." "Never mind," replied Mr. Jones, "I will get to the sinners. I never scald hogs until the water is hot."

His services created sensations in Cincinnati, Nashville, Chicago, Brooklyn, Baltimore, and Toronto, among other cities. Great congregations were stirred and many newspapers printed his sermons. The *Toronto Globe* commented: "Beecher was once described as irreverent; so was Spurgeon, so was Talmage, so was Moody, and so is Sam Jones. Is it possible that truth, religion and morality can be made too familiar to the people?" The *Cincinnati Enquirer* summed up the impression there: "Never before was such a religious awakening known in Cincinnati!" In St. Paul "he rushed through with a cyclone of Gospel truth and force, leaving the forces of the devil scattered and frightened, while Christians who had feared his coming and questioned his methods were left glad and thankful." Such is the newspapers' comment wherever he went to preach.

As a student in Vanderbilt University I heard him preach in the Auditorium and heard him speak in the Chapel at the University. In his sermons he denounced the city officers for their lax enforcement of the law and for immoral conditions in the city, until one wondered if he would be killed or run out of town. Then in the University Chapel he spoke to the students on "A Boy's Mother." In that talk was no slang, and the chaste language was so impressive that there were tears in all our eyes and hearts.

Through the forty-five years since those days I have remembered the appeal of this genius on the platform. As I try to sum up for myself the reasons for his great appeal I am sure of these things:

(1) He was deeply earnest and sincere in his zeal for moral reform.

(2) He was gifted of Heaven with an appealing voice and a keen, if homely, wit.

(3) His illustrations were drawn from everyday life as his thousands of hearers lived it.

(4) His early training as a lawyer gave him a sense of logical order and aided him in massing evidence which made him convincing in his arguments.

(5) His love for people and his concern for their realization of the finest and best made him a crusader for personal righteousness.

(6) His faith in God and God's forgiving mercy led him to believe that every broken human life could be made whole and every sinner a redeemed son of God.

In his last night service at Oklahoma City, just before he died, his sermon was on "Sudden Death." Speaking of his own death, he said, "When my last moment comes I will go home to God as happy as any schoolboy ever went home from school." A man who found two worlds so close together and God so near seemed to hundreds of baffled and confused humans a good guide to follow.

Ivan Lee Holt,
a Bishop of the Methodist Church

St. Louis, Missouri.

SAM
JONES

What is culture worth if it is but whitewash on a rascal? I would rather be in heaven learning my ABC's than sitting in hell reading Greek.

S. J.

1. ETERNAL DAMNATION

WE INVITE YOUR ATTENTION TO A VERY FAMILIAR TEXT, ONE that you have often heard quoted and perhaps frequently heard discussed from the pulpit:

What shall it profit a man if he gain the whole world and lose his own soul? And what will a man give in exchange for his soul?

It is strange, brethren, that while science and philosophy have been busying themselves so much with the doctrines and dogmas of Christianity—it is astonishing that they have never thought about how much good they would do this world if they would just stop all that and begin to answer a few questions of the New Testament Scriptures to the world.

Oh, what a vast benefit science and philosophy would be to humanity if they would just answer this question:

What will it profit a man if he gain the whole world and lose his own soul? Or, what will a man give in exchange for his soul?

Did you ever see an attempt on the part of any man to answer that question? Did you ever see a philosopher sit down to answer that other question: "How shall we escape if we neglect so great salvation?"

Now, if you notice the questions propounded by men to

God and His disciples you will recollect how quickly they were answered. Once a trembling jailer ran out into the presence of Paul and Silas and said: "Men and brethren, what must I do to be saved?"—the most important, infinitely important question in the universe—and in the twinkling of an eye St. Paul spoke out: "Believe on the Lord Jesus Christ and thou shalt be saved." You know, when the scribes and cunning Pharisees and shrewd Sadducees used to approach Christ with the most knotty questions in the universe, Jesus never said: "Wait till I come around again," or "Let me consult the authorities," or "Let me consult the encyclopedia," but in the twinkling of an eye always gave the answer to the most mighty problems and questions in the universe.

And now, while God answers immediately, I say to you that God propounds some questions to us that have been emblazoned on the pages of that book for thousands of years, and that we have never attempted to answer the question, "What shall it profit a man if he gain the whole world and lose his own soul?"

There are two things involved in this discussion: one is the world; the other is the soul.

This world is a multitudinous affair. It is a grand old world. There isn't a want of any physical and temporal nature that this world does not stand with outstretched, benevolent hands and say to me, "Here's what you want." If I want water, three-fourths of this world's surface is covered with water. If I want gold, the bowels of the earth are filled with gold. If I want books, the millions of shelves laden all around me bid me take off and read. If I want friends, the 1,400,000,000 of inhabitants upon the earth say, each one of them, "I will be your friend." If I want bread, the heavy laden harvest fields wave back to me a smile of plenty, which says, "Come and eat. Don't be hungry." If I want anything, and if I want everything, this old world stands up, with outstretched, generous hands, and says, "Here's what you want." I have no patience with the idea that this is a hard old world and that it is a bad old world. I don't like to have Christian people going about singing

This world's a howling wilderness, . . .

No howling wilderness! This is a grand world. It is just such a world as a benevolent, gracious Father would give His children to live in for three score years and ten. It is a glorious world, with all of its health-giving and life-perpetuating properties. This earth, with all its bountiful stores of remedies and life-giving eatables and life-perpetuating blessings, is a grand old world. There may be larger worlds and grander worlds than this, but this is a grand old world, brethren. What is it you want to-day as a man, as a mortal man, that this world doesn't stand ready to supply you? And one reason why I know God has prepared a grand immortal home for me is the fact that He has spread out such a grand world all around me for me to live in just for a few days. If this is the tent and tabernacle, what must be the everlasting halls of God?

I believe it was Talmage who used this illustration. He said: If a man is going to invest in property, about the first thing that man will do will be to look into the title. And after he has looked into the question of title, then the next thing will be the question of insurance, if it is town property. Then, the next question will be, How are others getting along who have made the investment? I believe Talmage said these are about the three questions that come up.

Now, suppose I go out as a merchant. I have spent my days largely in merchandising. I have accumulated a fortune, and now I want to retire to some beautiful country seat, where I may live in ease. I go out here a few miles and look over a magnificent farm, with its mansion, its outhouses, its creeks, its bottom lands, its table land, its woodlands, its all. It just suits me exactly. But, as a successful business man, I'm not going to count down one dollar for that land until I have come here and examined the book of deeds and book of liens and book of mortgages, to see if I can get a good title to that land.

Well, brother, when I look around this old world I see it is just the world for me, and about the first thing I'm going to look into is: What sort of title can I get to it? Do you know that a man may count down his soul for this world and in fifteen hours after he has made the trade death will come along with a writ of ejectment and say: "Off these premises! Get off forever!" And the poor fellow will pull out his deed; but death is blind and can't see to read it, and the poor fellow will say: "I have counted down my all for this piece of property," but death can't hear a word he says!

And how many men in my own knowledge have I seen build their nice houses and prepare for comfort and ease, and in less then twelve months after they have entered their new places, here is death coming to the door and knocking and walking in and saying: "Get out of the house and go to the cemetery." And maybe the fellow has in his pay almost every doctor in town, and he is begging the doctors for power against death; but death says: "You needn't send for the doctors. You needn't throw away any time. When I come for you I mean you have got to get off these premises." In my own town I can call to mind more than half a dozen men who, in middle age, had just built and fixed up their homes elegantly, and in less than twelve months from the time they entered their elegant homes were turned out of them and carried to the graveyard. And I know mansions in St. Louis that have had the black crape tied on the doorknob! What does it mean? It means—every black crape and every black veil in this world and every emblem of mourning mean, "You can't get any title to anything down here."

Oh, how true that is! Now, I like to see a man frugal and industrious and economical, and all that sort of thing, but, brethren, frugality and industry aren't always at the bottom of our desire to get hold of this world. There's many a man in this world that has accumulated and accumulated and accumulated, and you walk up to him and ask him: "Are you an old miser?"

"No," he says, "I'm no miser."

"Well, what are you piling it up this way for?"

"Well," he says, "I'll tell you. I'm laying up for Sally and the children. I'm determined that Sally and my children shall never endure the hardships I have undergone. I'm laying up for Sally and the children."

Yes, and if he could just see Sally and the children about twelve months after he has gone to the graveyard—Sally with her new teeth and the children in their fine turnout —the old fellow would be astonished how Sally and the children were getting along without him. He would that.

An old miser! Laying up everything and laying up everywhere and grasping in every direction, all to lay up and lay away, as he says, "for Sally and the children." And, my brethren, I love to see a man frugal, and I love to see him lay up, and I believe it is every man's bounden duty to lay up for a good wife and children, but when he passes the point where really, down in his heart, he is miserly and is not caring for wife and children, then, after he is dead and gone, his money will curse his children, and perhaps curse his wife. I have seen that. And I tell you the honest truth as I stand here and look on this congregation, if I had opportunity in this life—I don't know that I ever would—but if I had opportunity, I would lay by a competency for my wife to keep her from want—she has given the best years of her life to me and my children. I would lay by enough to make my wife comfortable in all her future age, but I wouldn't lay by a dollar in the world for one of my children. Do you know why? Because—listen!—if my children are any account, they don't need it, and if they are no account every dollar I give them will sink them.

I wish men would begin to learn that fact. An old miser died, and after he died a preacher told me he went there and stayed all night, and they put him upstairs, and he walked into the garret and saw a picture hanging with its face turned toward the wall. He turned the picture around and it was the old man's picture. They had sent it upstairs and turned its face to the wall! And that old man just spent his whole life laying up, as he said, "for Sally and the children," and look how they treated the old man!

Law, me! Look how Cornelius Vanderbilt was smirched all over in that trial after his death by his own legatees. Do you recollect it? Now, if a true, good, noble man has laid up for his wife, and laid up for his children, in harmony with God, I say all right. But I say a miser's money will curse him after he is dead and gone and curse his children, and perhaps his wife, when he is dead and gone. Some of the truest, noblest citizens have laid up a competency for their families, and their families are doing well today, and that is the proof that they laid it by right. But, brother, whenever a man ignores God and the rights of others and accumulates money in every direction, and then piles it up, as he says, simply for his family, that money will curse his family after he is dead and gone. We all know that is true. But if you will act in harmony with God, you can lay up all the money for your family you want to, and it will be a blessing to them after you are dead. But mind how you act out of harmony with God and grasp after this world!

And then I'll tell you another thing. It ain't only the rich that run after this world. There's many a poor fellow running after this world in this life and never gets any of it. I'm sorry for that sort of fellow. There's many a fellow out here on a farm with nothing but forty acres of poor land and an old stiff-eared mule; yet he stays right there and goes to hell for love of the world and love of money! He never has the money, but he loves it intensely. I use this old world and what it has got in it just like* I would use a walking-stick—to help me along to where I am going, and that is the only use I have got for it. And anything that is in my power that I can make help me upward as a stepping-stone to a better and higher life I want to use it.

This old world! You take A. T. Stewart, the richest money king in America. Just a week before his death it would have taken a hundred business men a hundred days to have told how much A. T. Stewart was worth. But now that he is dead, I want to find out how much he is worth, and a little fellow walks into his death chamber and takes a little tapeline out of his pocket and measures five feet ten inches one way, and eighteen inches the other way, and goes out here in the public cemetery and puts that measure on the ground, and there's the sum total of all A. T. Stew-

* In the South *like* is often used for *as* or *as if*.

art's possessions. Do you call that being rich? You just take the money princes of this world, that spend their life in gathering money and ignoring God, and I declare to you there are not enough millionaires in hell to-night, if the whole concern were to go into copartnership, to buy a drop of water to cool their parched tongues. Do you call that being rich? Do you call that acting wisely? You say that is for the best, do you? "As using and not abusing"?

That's it; and I reckon of all the insufferable conditions that pandemonium can offer to an immortal soul, as the poor fellow walks through the flames of damnation, is the consciousness: "I am money damned. I would have got to heaven if it hadn't been for filthy lucre. The devil tolled me into hell with nickels."

That's an awful state of things. Well, I have said frequently that if there is any sort of people in the world I want to see get to heaven, it's the poor white folks and Negroes. A poor fellow don't have anything in the world, and then to lay down and die and be damned forever is the most awful thought I ever had. These fellows, riding round, having a big time, and, ignoring God, they can sort of afford to be damned; but we poor white folks can't. But a man in hell with the consciousness, "I never had any fun up yonder, and then eternally burning here," it's a pretty bad joke on him, it seems to me.

This old world, how deceptive it is! And when you count down your soul for this world you cannot get a shadow of a title to it, and a wise man won't do that.

Well, then, you strike the question of insurance. You take a piece of property in this town that an insurance agent won't put a policy on, how much could you get for it on the market? There is not a man in the town that would buy it. Well, suppose you would take an insurance agent up to your house, and as you walked up toward the front gate the flames were bursting out from the cellar in your house, and the insurance agent says: "Mister, I can't insure that property, it is already on·fire down in the basement. Don't you see the flames bursting out?" Now, when you are going to get an insurance on this old world, the geologists tell us that it is already on fire down in the basement, already burning down there, and the chimneys for the under world—Vesuvius and Ætna. You see those burning volcanoes throwing out molten lava year after year.

I tell you, geology tells us a great truth when she tells us that this world is on fire down in the basement, and, God Almighty's word for it, she is going to burn up.

Astronomers have pointed their telescopes here and yonder, and they tell us that within the last few years thirteen worlds have disappeared. At first they looked like other worlds, after that they turned a deep red, showing they were on fire; and then they put on an ash color, showing they were burned to ashes; and then they disappeared, showing the very ashes were scattered abroad. Me get a title to it? I cannot get any insurance on it, and it is likely to be burned up any minute. I would not be fool enough to give any money for a thing of that sort, much less my immortal soul.

How about this being out in the trade? There is another thing. Did you ever talk with a fellow after he made a trade? You go to the city of Atlanta. On Peachtree Street is one of the prettiest lots in the city. It has never been built on, and you say to the real estate agent, "Why hasn't somebody built on this beautiful lot?" He will simply tell you, "Everybody who has had anything to do with this lot has had trouble about it. They buy a lawsuit when they buy this property. Nobody wants it." I have watched this old world pretty close, and every man who has had anything to do with this old world has got into trouble about it.

Did you ever notice that the most miserable man in the world to-night is the richest man in the world? I heard a fellow say once—he was rich, too—he said: "I said when I was young, all I wanted was $10,000, but," said he, "when I got $10,000, I wanted $20,000 twice as bad as I did that $10,000, and when I got $20,000, I wanted $40,000 four times as bad as I wanted the $20,000, and when I got $40,-000 I wanted $80,000 eight times worse than I wanted the $40,000. Oh," he said, "Jones, there is no use in talking; it is just like drinking salt water—the more you drink of it, the more you want of it, and the less room you have to hold it." And there's a good deal in that, too.

Laying up! And that's the reason men say, "I can't be religious; I am busy looking after the world; I am busy taking care of life; I am holding on to what I have got." Another old fellow told me: "I've spent my life now up to middle age making money, and I don't want to make another cent, but, Jones," he said, "I'll tell you the honest truth, it is harder to keep it after you get it than it was to make it to start with."

It's a pity for those fellows that have got it piled up and try to hold on to it, and everybody in the country wanting some of it. I'm sorry for them. Josh Billings says the old miser that has accumulated his millions and then sits down with his millions at last, without any capacity for enjoying it, reminds him of a fly that has fallen into a half-barrel of molasses. There you've got the picture just as complete as Josh Billings ever drew a picture.

I never had much money—never will, I reckon. I saw in the papers some time ago where a man had died in North Carolina, and left Sam Jones a wonderful legacy—and all that sort of thing. I was at home at the time. Several of my friends ran up with the paper, and said: "Sam, did you see this?"

"Yes."

"What are you going to do about it?"

"I ain't going to do anything."

"Well, I'd write on and tell him where I am."

Said I: "No, sir. I am getting on right well without a legacy, and God knows what I'd do if I had one. I am getting on so well without one that I don't want to fool with one."

Don't you see? I want you all to have legacies and live in fine houses, and I will go around and take dinner with you, and let you pay the taxes and servants, and I will enjoy the thing.

All things are yours—God said that—all things are yours, life and death, and Paul and Cephas, and everything is yours. I believe in the doctrine, not of communism, but of agrarianism. Everything is mine, thank God. I say I have never had much money—I reckon I never will—but I say this much: I have had money, and I have seen folks that did have money, and I think some here know what money will do, and I say a man is a fool, an immortal fool, that will sink his soul for money.

Right on this point, an incident occurred in a little town in Alabama, where I was born, before the war—Bowery, a little town off from the railroad. There were a great many wealthy planters lived all around it, and there were about eight or ten little stores there and one doggery saloon, and that was just about the time the lottery tickets came out and were popular, and several of those leading men invested in lottery tickets, and this barkeeper invested in one. The day after the drawing—there were no wires through the country then—they made up a plan and fixed it elegantly, and it was all arranged. So, the morning after the drawing, one of these wealthy farmers drove up at breakneck speed to the barroom, jumped out of his buggy, and ran in and said to the barkeeper: "I will give you $15,-000 for your ticket in the lottery." The barkeeper said, "What did I get? What did I draw?" "It makes no difference, I'll give you $15,000 for your ticket in the lottery." The barkeeper said he would not take it unless he knew what he drew.

And directly another drove up in his buggy and jumped out of the buggy and said to the barkeeper, "I will give you $25,000 for your ticket in the lottery." And the fellow says, "What did I draw?" "Well, I don't care what you drew, but I will give you $25,000 for your ticket." But the barkeeper would not take the money. And directly here was another driving up, another one, and they just came on and on, until they ran the ticket up to $85,000, and he would not take it.

And they all came out, and the fellow locked his back door and locked his front door and put off for home and never came back any more that day.

And next morning he walked up town to the post office, walked in there, and the post that morning brought the news from the lottery, and he saw what the news was and saw that he had not drawn anything, and he walked right back through that crowd, and as he passed through there was a suppressed titter of laughter, and he walked on a step or two and turned right around and walked back and faced them, with a mingled look of resentment and sadness and disappointment and joy in his face, and he turned to them, and said: "Gentlemen, hear me. Before God, as an honest man, I tell you I am glad I didn't get a cent."

Said he: "I left my grocery yesterday about 11 o'clock, just as certain that I had that capital prize—I could not have been more certain if I had it in my hand, and I went home believing I had it, and I commenced talking with my wife, and we just sit there all day; and sit there all night long last night, and never slept one wink, talking about what we'd do with that money, and," he said, "as God is my judge, the most miserable time I ever spent in my life was since yesterday morning. I am glad, before God, that I didn't get that money—I am. I was rich yesterday and last night, just as rich as if I had it in my hand, and I am poor now. I'd rather be poor a thousand times than rich once."

Do you get the idea? Now, that fellow tried that once and knew what he was talking about.

What is this world? A man will die now and leave his daughters $100,000 apiece, and another man dies next door and he leaves his daughters not a cent. Those poor girls go to sewing hard every day, working on a machine, and those rich girls go keeping up with the fashion. Now, watch them three years from that time, and the fashionable girls look sallow and pale and bloodless and nearly dead on their feet, and there are the red, rosy, healthy vigorous girls. It will kill a girl quicker having to keep up with the fashion than if she sews all day for a living.

What do you want it for? How many in this world are making a fatal mistake right at that point? What do you want with it—to curse you, to curse your families?

And in my own State I can go around the horseshoe bend of one of our rivers, in the finest plantations in that State, and I can take those plantations one after another—the old people died during the war—and I am saying the truth to-night when I say that nine out of ten of their boys have already filled drunkards' graves and drunkards' hells.

Twenty thousand dollars, a hundred thousand dollars, will buy nine boys out of ten a through ticket to hell, and they will invest in it the first thing they do and check their baggage right through, and heaven and earth cannot stop them. Don't you know that is so?

If my father, instead of turning to me in his dying hour and bidding me meet him in heaven, had spent his life accumulating money and had turned over $25,000 to me when he died, I'd have been in the pit this moment.

God bless you, brothers, show your children there is something better than money, and better than this world, and better than all the surroundings; show them there is a God and an eternity, and that character is worth more than gold. "What will it profit a man if he gain the whole world . . . ?"

If you get it all and lose your soul, what are you profited?

Well, whoever got the whole world? Whoever got one millionth part of this world? Some fellows think they are rich if they are worth $100,000. Well, what is $100,000 compared to Vanderbilt's fortune? Or, if you owned Vanderbilt's fortune, what is that compared to the city of New York? And the city of New York, if you owned it all, what is that compared with America? And if you owned all America, what is that compared with the whole world? And if you owned the whole world down here, I expect if you could put two such worlds as this in your pocket and go to the dog star, and stay all night, that you wouldn't have enough to pay your hotel bill in the morning. And, after all, what is there in this world that takes away so much of our time and so much of our talent and so much of our energy? And how foolish it is!

A father in one of the Southern cities said to me: "Oh,

26

two of my boys are dissipated, and my money will ruin my boys, and I know it."

Said I: "You say you've got money enough to ruin them both?"

"Yes."

"And you are certain it will ruin them?"

Said he: "Yes."

Said I: "I'll tell you how to dodge that thing."

Said he: "How?"

"Well," said I, "give me this afternoon $20,000 apiece of those two boys' money for the orphan home out here, and you go home to-night and say to Tom and Henry, 'I have given Sam Jones $20,000 of each of your money, and the very next time you get drunk I am going to give him $40,000 of each of your money; and, further, on your third drunk I will make him a deed for that orphans' home for every dollar I have got.' "And," said I, "you will straighten them boys straight out—you will that."

And before my money should damn my children, I say to you to-night, I would give it all to the orphan homes of the country. Well, as I said, I told him what he should do with his money, and—well, strange to say, he never gave me a cent. I am afraid he will be in the pit before his boys are.

You can go down among the rich bottoms of the Missouri and Mississippi rivers and there you will find the most impure water and the most malarious atmosphere in the country. You can go up among the old red hills of Georgia, and the clearest sparkling water you ever saw gurgles up through the old red clay, and the sweetest atmosphere blows over the old red hills of Georgia. Among the rich of this earth is the most corruption, and the most wickedness, and the most guilt. Among the poor of the earth you will find the sweetest virtues and the noblest characters. Let us live among the poor. Let us have a good atmosphere and good water.

And I will tell you, brothers, that when a man gets drunk on money he is gone. You preachers are not candid with him. You do not tackle him as you should. When an old fellow gets drunk with whisky, his friends go to him and say: "Look here, old fellow, you are going to the devil. I want you to quit and keep straight." His wife pleads with him. The minister pleads with him. Everybody pleads with him. But when a fellow gets drunk with money, bless you, his wife does not say anything about it. She enjoys the "creetur" herself; she does not say, "Husband, you are going to perdition." The preacher does not tackle him; he is afraid to. There's many a man in this town drunk with money. Have you brethren been up to tell them, "You are drunk with money and the devil will get you"? You never tackle them. You just say, "I want the favor of these old rich fellows, because I know if I bother them they will get mad with me, and neutralize my action and neutralize my power, and I cannot do anything," and they think: "The best thing to do is to let the old fellows alone. I don't want to antagonize them, but just make them pay their way."

Oh, sirs, when a man gets drunk on money, nobody bothers him then. He just goes on and on, and to perdition he goes forever.

Oh that you all could see what keeps you out of the church and from God! That is the price you have placed on your immortal soul.

Now, a word in conclusion. The soul—that is the other thing. There is the world and here is the soul. Now what?

My soul, with its immortal interest; my soul, that shall live forever; my soul, that will shake off this body by and by, and lay it aside as a child does its doll after it has done playing with it; my soul, that shall throw this body down and fly away from it; shall I give my immortal soul for this world? No, sir, I cannot do that. What then? I will give my soul to Christ. He is worthy of it; He died to save it.

Yonder is a parliament. Adam has just fallen and subjected the whole race to death, and now the reverberating thunders of God's wrath are heard athwart the whole moral universe, and the announcement is made in that parliament, "Adam—Man—has fallen. The great federal head of the race has sinned and fallen," and a voice from the great I Am spoke out, "Who will take man's redemption on his shoulders and bring him back to life?" I imagine the archangel stands up in that presence and shakes his snowy wings, and says: "This task is too great for me." I imagine Gabriel might stand up and say, "I shall blow the trumpet that will wake the dead, but this task is too great for me." But all at once there was one who stood up in that presence and said: "I will take man's redemption on my shoulders." And the angels began to wonder, and it has been the cause of increasing wonder ever since, that He should become the Redeemer, that He should become man that He might redeem the race and be our Saviour.

Brothers, you saw some years ago that a ship in the Atlantic Ocean sprang a leak away down in the bottom of her hull. The announcement that the ship had sprung a leak was made by the captain, and the pumps were got to work, but they could not pump out the water as fast as it entered by the leak. The only hope for the safety of the vessel was that someone would give his life in order to stop the leak. Volunteers were asked for, and one man spoke up, "I will go down and stop the leak." He went down and down—to the upper, then the lower, and then the third deck, and then he reached down into the water and worked there until completely exhausted. The pumps begin to work, and by and by the old ship grew lighter, and by and by the captain said: "The leak is stopped, but let us go down and see about our friend." They went down to the third deck and saw his body floating on the water. They brought him up and embalmed his body, and when land was reached they carried it ashore and buried it. And the spot was marked by a tombstone on which is the epitaph: "This friend gave his life that all of us might live." And the names of those he saved are all engraved below. And they bless the memory of that man and say: "If he had not died we should have been lost."

And yonder is the old ship Humanity, and now the waves of God's wrath and judgment begin to pitch and toss her and drive her on the rocks, and she is about to go down forever, when the Son of God sees her; and I see him come from the shining shores of heaven, as swift as the morning light, and throw His arms around this old, sinking ship. She carries him under three days and nights, and He brings her to the surface on the third morning; and then God grasps the stylus and signs the Magna Charta of man's salvation, and then at the blessed moment it is written: "Whosoever believeth in the Son of God shall not perish, but have everlasting life."

I will give my life to Christ; He gave His life for me, and He is worthy of it.

Down South, before the war, we used to put a slave on the block and sell him to the highest bidder. Sometimes he would run away and we could not get him on the block, but we would sell him on the run. "How much for him running away?" Well, brothers, when God Almighty turned this world over to Jesus Christ He turned it over on the run, running away from God, running away to hell and death, and the Lord Jesus Christ came as swift as the morning light and overtook this old world in her wayward flight, threw His arms around her and said: "Stop, stop, let us go back to God. Let us go back."

Oh, Jesus Christ, help every man here to say, "I will go back. I have strayed long enough. I will go back now." Will you, brothers? God help every man to say, "This night I have taken my last step in the wrong direction, and have turned round." That is just what God wants sinners to do—to turn round—to turn round. Will you to-night say, "God being my helper, I will stop. I will turn my attention to heavenly things and eternal things. I will look after my soul, if I starve to death"? Will you do that?

I know preachers who look as sad and solemn as if their Father in heaven was dead, and hadn't left them a cent.

S. J.

2. ALL THINGS WORK
TOGETHER FOR GOOD

And we know that all things work together for good to them that love God, to them who are the called according to his purpose.—ROMANS 8:28.

WE CAN SAY THERE IS BUT ONE SINGLE EXCEPTION IN ALL the universe to the truth of this utterance, and God makes that exception all through His book. Everything in this universe works together for the good of those that love God, except sin. There is nothing in sin or of sin, or about sin or around sin or above it or beneath it, or connected with it in any way, that can ever work to anybody's good. What you have done that is wrong, what you ought to have done that you did not do, God can never make work to your good. If you have stayed away from a prayer meeting, God can never make that work to your good. If you have neglected your duty, God can never make that neglect work for your good. There is no provision of grace to make up for anybody what he has lost from the neglect of duty. "All things work together for good to them that love God."

Now, recollect, if you are a Christian and love God, everything you cannot help, everything you would have warded off if you could, everything you would have conquered if you could, everything in this life, works together for good, except sin, and God Himself cannot make sin work for anybody's good, because sin is the reversal, the throwing-out of gear of the machinery of our nature. When we begin to go wrong we reverse the machinery of our nature and run it backwards. You can no more work for God when you reverse the machinery of your nature than you can make your sewing-machine sew when you run it backwards. One is as impossible as the other. All things work for good when you are running in harmony with God and in a line with God; for, after all, religion is nothing more than harmony with God. When you walk up to your piano, and touch a key in that elegant instrument, and that key is out of tune, and of harmony, that key is out of harmony not only with the rest of the keys of the piano, but out of harmony with everything in the universe that is in harmony. But when the piano tuner walks up to that piano and opens it, and takes out his instruments and works away at that particular string until he gets it in harmony, then that key is in harmony with everything in the universe. And religion is getting in harmony with God. Then everything moves along harmoniously, adjusting and setting the Ten Commandments to music. Is it not so? When God bids me do this or that He touches a chord in my nature in sympathy with His own divine heart, and then we are in harmony with all. God wills and wishes, and He will make everything in this universe conduce to our present and eternal happiness. "And ye know that all things work together for good to them that love God."

There is the text. There are three classes of people here, and these three classes represent the whole world. The first class we mention are those that know they do love God. Thank God, there are such persons on the face of the earth—persons who know they do love God. There is another class here, and those in that class do not love God, and about nine-tenths of us make up the third class, persons who do not know whether they love God or not. Sometimes they think they love Him. Sometimes they think they do not. Nine-tenths of the world are made up of don't-know-what-to-thinks. Oh, how numerous they are! But what is the use of going on in that way? When I was a ten-year-old boy, if you asked me, "Do you love your mother?" I would reply: "Yes, sir, I do."

"Do you know why?"

"Because when I do what mother says for me to do I feel good about it, and when I go to do something mother told me not to do I feel bad about it."

"Well, what other reason?"

"I love her, and I love to hear her name reverently used and kindly used."

"Well, what other reason?"

"It makes me feel bad for anyone to speak unkindly and irreverently of my mother."

Now you ask me, "Are you a Christian?"

"Yes."

"Do you love God?"

"Yes."

"How do you know you do?"

"Because when I do like God tells me I feel so good about it."

"How else do you know it?"

"Because when I do something He told me not to do, I feel as bad about it as I can."

"How else do you know it?"

"It does me good to hear people praise God and speak reverently of Him, and it gives me a horror to hear anyone blaspheme Him."

35

I have as many reasons why I love God as I had why I loved my mother.

The love of God is not necessarily an emotional feeling. I hear people talk a heap about feeling that they love God. I never stop to see whether I have got feelings or not. I never inquire about that. Some people say they never want to do anything unless they feel like it. I have seen preachers that are always gadding about, and are extremely anxious that all the members of their congregations shall be visited. Then there are preachers whose minds and hearts are in their church, and they would rather be whipped than go and see anybody. This brother deserves a thousand times more credit than Brother Gadabout. The Lord knows I feel sorry for one of those pitty-patty brothers who are always drumming all over their congregation, seeing old sister So-and-So, you know—always gadding about. If pastoral visiting would have saved this town it would have been saved long ago. God never said that people should be saved by pastoral visiting. He said: "The preaching of the gospel is the power of God unto salvation."

And I have a great deal more respect for the brother who would rather talk and preach than go and see anybody than I have for the brother who would rather be running around all the time. I tell you how I feel about it. I do not care whether a minister ever puts a foot in my house all the year round or not; but I will say one thing: When my wife and children visit my pastor I want him to preach enough solid truth to keep them going the whole week, instead of running and gadding about and getting in my wife's way and keeping things disarranged all the week looking for the preacher.

I want my preacher to let my family visit him at the house of God. I never saw people that quarreled about the pastor not visiting them that amounted to much, anyhow. If you treat a preacher right, and give him a good square meal every time he calls, he ain't got any more sense than to come back again. If a preacher don't come to see you it is your own fault. Christ told His disciples when they went to a place, to go to one house and put up there and not to be running about all over creation. He knew what He was talking about. But if I could not preach much I would make it up in visiting. You quit bothering your preacher about coming to see you, and help him in his work. If he has one thousand members in his church, you make yourself useful and help him to look after the other 999. I used to have some members of my church everlastingly at me to visit them. One family bothered me more than any of the others, and when I did make a call I made it a jumping, bouncing class-meeting, and they never bothered me any more.

Now, I branched off from the subject I was discussing. I say, whether we feel like it or not, let us say: "I am going to do what I consider is right." I am not inquiring this afternoon whether there is an emotional feeling toward God in my heart. What has Jesus Christ said? "Hereby ye know that ye love me because ye feel that ye do so"? No, He never said that; He said: "Hereby ye may know that ye love me, because ye keep my commandments."

God, love, and loyalty are synonymous in this sense. "Hereby ye may know that ye love me, because ye keep my commandments."

Loyalty to the right—absolute eschewing of the wrong— is proof that ye love God, to them that love God; or, in other words, this text might read this way: "All things work together for good to them that keep the commandments of God."

That is about the practical meaning of the text. Well, now, if I am loyal to God straight out, through and through, then the promise is: "All things shall work together for good."

Well, I might stop here, but I wonder what that word "good" means. Suppose we give it this interpretation: "All things shall work together for the riches of God's people."

Temporal riches—temporal prosperity! Why, if it had read that way there would not have been a word of truth in it, because, generally speaking, God's people are poor people. And yet I may say that the richest man this world ever saw, Abraham, was the best man the world ever saw. But, generally speaking, God's people are a poor people.

I met this summer a millionaire who went down in the fearful financial stringency this year, and he was a good, generous, noble man, and he had gone down and surrendered everything, even his house and lot. When I was talking to him I said, "Oh, my brother, I do not understand how it is you were ruined. You were very liberal with your money. You have built churches and parsonages, and given to the church. You were very liberal. How is it you went down in this fearful financial wreck?"

"Well," he said, "I will tell you. God knows I tried to do my duty with my money. I gave it as liberally as the gushing of a river. I am conscious of that. After the last dollar was swept away I got a cruel letter from a creditor —a cruel letter, and it almost literally broke my heart. I went into my room and I knelt down on my knees with my Bible in my hand and I said: 'Oh, my gracious God, I am ruined financially, and my friends are pouncing on me and saying the bitterest words! Oh, my God! I will never get up off my knees until you explain this thing to me I do not understand.' I prayed there with that Bible in my hand, and when I opened it the first line I saw was this: 'How hardly shall they that have riches enter into the kingdom of heaven.' I just jumped off my knees and clasped my hands together, and said, 'Glory be to God, that is reason enough.' " And he said: "If I am poor I am going to do my duty."

Then, most people cannot stand prosperity. Now, if you are going to be rich and religious both at the same time and place, all right, and if ever you get to heaven you will wear a bright crown there; no doubt about that. But I will say one thing to you, you had better look out along that line. Some folks think I have some spite against rich folks, like all poor white trash, but I have no spite against anybody. If there is anybody good to me it is the rich. If there is anybody kind to me it is the rich. I think so much of the rich people of this country that I shall not let the devil get them if I can help it, and I am going to talk to them when I feel like it.

How many genuinely scriptural, pious rich women do you know in town? I do not mean how many belong to the church. I know the church will get them in, and it's glad to get them, religion or no religion. I ain't talking about that. How many genuinely scriptural, devoted, pious rich women have you got in your city? How many pure, noble, consecrated, self-sacrificing, pious men who are millionaires have you got in your city? Now, I never said there were not any. I never said how many. I ask you how many.

When I was in St. Joseph preaching, there was a story in the morning papers to the following effect: "Jones is not doing much with the Thirty."

The next morning I would see: "The Thirty were pretty well represented at the meeting."

I said to my friends: "What does this 'Thirty' business mean?"

"Oh," they said, "there are in this city thirty millionaires, thirty men of the world, worth over $1,000,000 each." These things were against them.

Some of those men I found to be true, noble, Christly and generous, but those who were not, we did not make much impression upon. One of the old millionaires who professed religion joined the church. Afterwards I said to him: "Well, my brother, you have disposed of your soul, have you given it to God? But you have a heap harder job left before you—what to do with your money. You had better begin to unload now. Shell out now, for if you are ever damned it will be by your money. Mark what I tell you."

If I had one-tenth of the money some members of the church have in this town and I did not do any better with it than they do, the devil would get me as certainly as my name is Sam Jones. And if you have got as much sense as I have and you don't get up from where you are, the devil will get you, too.

Prosperity! God never said: "All things should work together for the prosperity of God's people." They could not stand it. Some folks could not go to heaven out of a three-story house. That's a fact. I do not say I am one of those who could. I never tried it and never will, I reckon. Prosperity! I do not want anything to come between me and my loyalty to God. I like Agur's prayer:

Give me neither poverty nor riches. Give me not poverty, lest I steal: give me not riches, lest I be puffed up and say, Who art thou, Lord?

The medium is best. Let me have "sufficient unto the day," with the blessed assurance that I shall dwell in the land and shall be fed.

God never said, "All things shall work together for the health of God's people."

I think some of the most afflicted people I ever met in this life have been the best people I ever met, and I think sometimes most of us would get along better if we were sick more. Take an ordinary Methodist, now a backslider, and strike him down with a six weeks' spell of typhoid fever, and you can do more to get him better spiritually than by preaching 500,000 sermons. Take and shake a sinner over a coffin and turn him loose, and he will hit the ground running every time.

David said: "It was good for me that I was afflicted." It is a mighty hard matter to keep a big, fat, sleek Methodist straight, but get us down for a day to where we are pretty near to death and eternity and it has a good effect. It is wholesome.

Just as was said of Jenny Lind. After Goldsmith first heard her sing and walked out of the opera house, somebody said: "Goldsmith, how did you like her singing?" He said: "Well, there was a harshness about her voice that needs toning down. If I could marry that woman, break her heart and crush her feelings, then she could sing." And it is said that afterwards, when he did marry her and broke her heart and crushed her feelings, Jenny Lind sang with the sweetest voice ever he listened to, so sweet that the angels of God would almost rush to the parapets of heaven to catch the streams of the sweetest voice earth ever possessed.

Sometimes violets send forth their sweetest odors when

41

crushed beneath the foot. Some of the most religious people have been the most deeply afflicted; and if there is one prayer I have prayed from the depths of my heart it is, "Lord, if I am to save my soul at any cost; if I am to lie on a bed of pain for thirty years, if that is necessary, let me begin now and suffer till I draw my last breath rather than to be joyous and healthy in this life and then enter into the other world and into a life of interminable suffering. Lord, whatever is necessary to save my soul, let it come on me. Save my soul, good Lord, at any cost to me." That is the way we ought to pray.

God never said all things should work together for the health of God's people. He never said that. I used to think when I first became religious that if I got sick or my wife got sick, "That's a sign God don't love me." But now I know that God loves me with all His great heart.

It is not said, "All things shall work together for the honor and popularity of God's people." No, sir, when the disciples preached the truth, only one of them died a natural death, it is said. Those that loved to preach the truth rotted to death in dungeons or were burned at the stake or stoned. It is not a very popular thing to be an earnest, zealous Christian. It is not. God never said "All things are working together for the popularity of God's people."

You take a popular preacher, a preacher whom everybody likes, whom the gamblers like, the liars like, the drunkards like, and I say that whenever liars and gamblers and hypocrites and backslidden members like me I'll tell the Lord: "I am wrong. I know I am. There is something wrong about this thing."

I have noticed another thing. You recollect the Pharisees and Sadducees had no use for one another. They hated each other, but when Christ came along they clubbed together and let in on Him. Here is a backsliding Baptist sister, and there is a backsliding Methodist sister. They have no use for each other under ordinary circumstances, but when a preacher comes along and knocks the bark off of them they join against him, and it is astonishing how thick they get. They meet at the theater or at the card table, and there are a great many places and a great many points on which they agree, and wherever they meet they join in the fight against this one or that one.

Now, I believe in voting. This country is running a good deal on voting, and I want every lady in this house that enjoys religion, and has got cares at home, who goes to the theater, who shines at sociable parties and dances—just square dances, she has not cut the corners of the thing yet —I want every lady here that really enjoys religion, and goes to these places and plays cards and dances, to stand up. I want to see you. Stand up, every one of you! If I were one I would stand up and be laughed at and say: "Here is one."

(No one responded to the invitation.)

But I will tell you what they will say now. They will say: "I don't enjoy religion. I will admit that. I have got religion, but I don't enjoy it." Now, listen to me: There is but one reason why nobody enjoys religion, and that is because they have not got any to enjoy. It is the most enjoyable thing a fellow ever struck, and the question with me would be, How can I keep from enjoying it? Got religion, but don't enjoy it!

The popularity of God's people. He never said, "All things shall work together for the worldly honors of God's people." He never said that. I am glad the Lord's people don't take many honors in this world, the way it goes now. I am glad they don't take any good Christian and run him for president, the way they run them now. I am glad of that. I tell you, if a man was all right and they ran him for president, wouldn't they smirch him? Take Blaine and Cleveland. Ten years of close application of warm water and soft soap would not wash off the smirching and vituperation that was thrown on those two men in their last race. If what was said against those two men was true they ought both to be in the chain gang. I am glad the Lord's people do not have to have things in that way. I don't want to be president if they put more mud on me before I get there than I can wash off while I am there.

Worldly honors! They are not for God's people. What *does* this mean—"All things work for good"?

What is this "good"? It ain't health. It ain't happiness. It ain't prosperity. It ain't worldly honors. What is it the Lord means here? Now, let us come to the true text for a moment: "All things work together for the salvation of them that love God."

Salvation is the greatest good this earth ever heard of or could experience. Now, I can see into the text and see into a thousand things. "All things work together for the salvation." For the persistent, eternal salvation of them that love God. A heap of strange things happen in this world, sister. You say, "Well, I cannot see to save my life how the loss of my husband could work for my good." "I cannot see how the loss of my sweet child can work for my good." "I cannot see how the loss of every dollar of our property can work for my good." Oh, how strange things have happened! Well, now, you see that clock on the mantel at home. You walk up and look at that clock. You take it down and look at the dial, and look at the works, which must be put together by a clock-maker. I took my clock to pieces once and after I had put it together again I had sufficient wheels left to make another clock. I could not get it together. It had been made by a clock-maker, and only a clock-maker could put the wheels in their proper places again.

When I look at the works of a clock I say, "Well, well, all those wheels cannot be necessary." There is one big wheel turning slowly and another one fast. There is a great big one turning backward and a little one forward. I say a clock like that cannot keep time. I put the dial back and the clock ticks on and strikes the hours, and I say, "It does keep time. I do not care how it looks." Now, God sets up in heaven the largest clock of all, and we cannot see the machinery. There is health and peace in my family. Well, that is a little wheel moving forward. The last dollar of my property is swept away. Well, that's a big wheel turning backward, but all things work for you and work harmoniously in one direction for your present good and eternal salvation.

When I was at Columbus, Ga., I walked through an immense cotton factory. I was shown all the machinery—that which cut the hoops to go round the raw cotton, that which picked the cotton, and I followed one machine after another, from one floor to another. I watched some machinery carding cotton, others pulling it onto reels. At times I would say: "Look here, surely this is not the way to make cloth. If I did not want to make cloth, I would do just like you are doing." But when we got to the last machine, on the fourth floor, there was a pile of cotton cloth bundled up, ready for the market. I looked down the line of machines, and said, "Every machine in this factory works together for cloth"; and, sister, by and by, when you step

45

into the heavenly gates, you will look back and say: "Everything in my life worked for good." Oh, how true these things are!

My father used to say: "My son, if you do that I will correct you." When I got off by myself I said: "Papa is so cruel to me. Sometimes he whips me for doing some things, and if ever I get grown up I am going to ask papa what made him do that. But I was not eighteen when I found that my father had corrected me for things that would have ruined me if I had been left alone. And when you get to heaven you will say: "God brought me to salvation the only way He could have brought me safely this far." "All things work together for good . . ."

A man once gave me this illustration of the text. He said he was sitting out under a tree in a garden eating a biscuit, when he saw a little ant climbing on the plank. He watched it, and said: "I reckon this little ant is in search of food." He had dropped a crumb, but the little ant was going in the opposite direction to it. He put his finger in the way of the ant to direct it to the crumb, and the little thing seemed to lose patience and want to quarrel with him, and it seemed to say: "Why do you stop me? I am hunting food for my young." The ant started off in another direction, and he dropped his finger again in front of the little ant, which seemed to be madder than before, and it seemed to say: "Oh, you great intelligent creature, why do you stop me? I am hunting food for my young." He dropped his finger in front of the ant again and again, and each time it seemed to say, "Why do you stop me? I am in earnest search of food for my young." He said he dropped his finger in front of the ant until he directed it to the crumb, and when it picked up the crumb it seemed to say, "I am so glad you put me in the way of finding this. Here is more food than I could have found in a month if you had left me alone."

In this world, when we are moving in the wrong direction, down comes the providential finger of God, and you say, "I know I have the worst luck of anybody." And we stand and quarrel with God and ourselves. We start out in another direction, and just about the time we think we are about to succeed, down comes God's providential finger, and we say, "Just look at that!" In this way God drives us right to the gate of heaven, and when we walk in there we say: "Glory be to God. If we had been left alone we would have gone to perdition, but He has driven me right to the joys of everlasting life."

Providence means going before. Providence. I believe in Providence as strongly as I believe in anything. Here is a wagon train moving westward. A horseman lopes ahead, picks out the camping place, buys the provender for the stock, and arranges everything. That man was the providence of the wagon train. Providence to go on ahead, to arrange and plan everything. Now, let us in God's providence from this time say, "I will go along and trust in God that everything will work together for good." "Though he fall he shall not be utterly cast down, for the Lord upholdeth his hand."

I hold a baby's hand as it walks. Its foot strikes something and it falls with a force that would crush its face. But I hold up the baby by the hand and I say, "Baby, I am so glad you had my hand. If you had not held it you would have ruined your little face on the rocks." I have sometimes gone along and fallen, and I have thought I was gone forever, but the Lord had my hand and held me up, and I say, "Bless the Lord! If He had not held my hand I should have fallen down into eternal despair."

47

One day my two little boys ran ahead of me on the sidewalk. Directly I noticed they were back again, holding by my fingers. "Well," I thought, "what does this mean?" I looked ahead and saw a few steps in advance a lot of cattle on the sidewalk. When they saw the cattle the boys had run back and got hold of my fingers, and they continued to laugh and play, as much as to say: "We were afraid when we saw those cattle alone, but now we would laugh and play if all the cattle in the world were here, for we are with father." Let me say to you, If you have got hold of God's hand you are safe. When dangers and disappointments beset you, you laugh and rejoice. Lord help and bless us, and save us.

The devil has no better servant than a preacher who is laying feather-beds for fallen Christians to light on.

S. J.

3. BE NOT WEARY IN WELL-DOING

WE INVITE YOUR ATTENTION TO THE 9TH VERSE OF THE 6th chapter of St. Paul's Epistle to the Galatians:

And let us not be weary in well-doing, for in due season we shall reap if we faint not.

This exhortation may be wisely and prayerfully considered by us now. Moral forces necessarily move slowly. This city has been wicked for forty years, and if you think it can be brought to God in a day you know nothing of moral forces and how they operate. This exhortation comes in with a good deal of force upon us here to-night: "Let us not weary in well-doing, for in due season—"

There's the promise—"for in due season we shall reap it if we faint not."

Well, now, this very verse, like some verse of almost every chapter in the Bible, is a key to the whole chapter. This chapter before us is a great palace of Scripture truth and this text is a key. I take this text and I walk up to the front door of this great palace of truth and I unlock the front door and walk in, and the first thing my eye falls upon is this: "Brethren, if a man be overtaken in a fault,

51

ye which are spiritual, restore such an one in the spirit of meekness."

Then I find from the lesson of to-night that the first well-doing of every Christian man is to ignore himself, and that of every good man to live for others. If there is anything incompatible with Christianity it is selfishness. If there is anything that Christianity fights and would have you and me put out of the way it is selfishness. And hell itself is nothing but pure, unadulterated, concentrated selfishness. There is not an intolerable element in hell itself that has not in it every element of selfishness. No man is in a position to do for others until he can get himself out of the way. The greatest man I ever saw was the most unselfish man. The smallest man I ever saw was the most selfish. There is a little preacher on a small circuit in Georgia who, when I walk up into his presence grows and expands and develops, and I commence to whittle and whittle down until I feel like a mole-hill by a mountain, and do you know why that man seems so great and I seem so small? It is because when I look into his face I look into the face of the most unselfish man my eyes ever looked upon. Why, he don't care anything for himself. His last thought at night is: "How can I benefit somebody to-morrow?" and his first thought in the morning, "Where may I go and what may I do to benefit some one to-day?"

This world is run on selfish principles. "How much enjoyment may I get out of this, and how much profit out of that, and how much will I lose by the other." Selfishness always defeats itself—never carries its point. You let a man live for himself, and lay up money for himself, and provide for himself, and let all the world go. "Let all the world go, but I am going to lay up for myself." Why such a man as that defeats his very end. In our State a man spent

52

his life laying up for his old age. He said, "I'm never going to want. I'm going to lay up for my old age." He laid up $200,000, and to illustrate his state of mind, one of his neighbors was over at his house one day, and they were talking about one thing and another, and directly the neighbor said, "Well, how are you off for meat?" The old rich fellow said, "Well, I've got a smokehouse full now and hogs enough to make me meat this fall, and pigs enough to make it full afterwards, but what in the world I am to do after that I can't tell!" That old fellow was starving to death with three year's rations on hand.

Selfishness! Live for self, love for self, work for self, and let all the world go. Now, that sort of spirit is at enmity with Christianity, and I assure you that Christianity is at enmity with a spirit like that. Our Lord taught us a great lesson in unselfishness. Do you know that around all the broad acres of this world Jesus of Nazareth never staked Him off a single acre and told the world, "That's mine"? Do you know that amid all the palaces of earth Jesus looked out and said: "The foxes have holes, the birds of the air have nests, but I have nowhere to lay my head"? Do you know that, amid all the coin on earth, Jesus, when pressed for His taxes, sent His disciples to a fish's mouth to get money to pay them? We see that unselfish One as He arises in the morning, and after a simple breakfast at the home of Mary and Martha, walks out on the streets of the city, and over here He is giving sight to a blind man, and over there He is healing the sick, and over there He is cleansing a leper, and in the afternoon He meets a widow bearing her son to the tomb to bury him, and He takes the son by the hand and lifts him back into his mother's loving arms, and, amid the shouts of praise from the mother's lips, He presses His way until He reaches the farthest suburbs of the city, and then He stops by the road-side and sits down and leans His head on His aching arm, and says: "This is the first time I have thought of myself since I got up this morning. I have just been thinking about others; how I could benefit others; how I could do for others; I have been hunting the blind; I have been seeking the sick; I have been comforting the disconsolate." Oh, Christ! Thy life was written in a single sentence: "He went about doing good." And the man who is most like Christ is the man that spends most of the hours of his life just like Christ did, going about doing good.

Now, the first lesson of this text tells us:

Brethren, if a man be taken in a fault, ye which are spiritual go and restore such an one in the spirit of meekness, consider-ing thyself also lest thou be tempted.

I used to think there was a great deal of difference, after all, in our churches and in the membership of our churches. I have thought, after all, we have got our first-class members and our second-class members and our tenth-rate members, and all that sort of thing. But, breth-ren, the great trouble is, we can hardly find a whole man among us. We have got pieces enough to make a thousand, but they won't fit. We file and saw and chip and plug, and yet here we are to-day without a whole man in the city of St. Louis.

Now, we say: "There are a great many different sorts of members in the church." I grant you that. There is one brother. He says: "I declare, if you don't turn out these dancing members, I'm going to quit the church. I won't live in a church with dancing members." You see, he don't dance. But I tell you what he will do every day—loan his money at twenty per cent. interest; and God says that the man who will do that ain't fit for the church, and will

54

never go to heaven. Here's another brother. He's got no money to loan, and he despises dancing, but you can tote him right into hell with a demijohn, he does love liquor so. Here's another member of the church. He don't drink and don't lend money at usury, and don't dance, but he will skin you nine times out of ten when you go to trade with him, and I want to say this: You will never know how much real, genuine scriptural hell fire there is in a good trade till you get to hell. And I tell you another thing: We can sort of put up with a fellow that sins like we sin, but when he does something we won't do, we are ashamed of him right straight. I declare, I never see a man doing anything wrong that I don't get off to myself, and bury my face in my hands, and say: "Look a-here! You may not sin like that man, but are you not doing something just as bad in the sight of God?" I say we can put up with a man as long as he sins like we do, but when he does something we won't do, then we'll fall out with him right there, and say: "That man won't do."

Now, I like this position. If there is in your church an incorrigible backslider, then every man in it has backslidden. You say: "How do you know that?" Well, sir, the spirit that will make you neglect a backslidden brother, I don't care what else you do, or what else you don't do, that spirit will make you backslide in spite of all you can do. For if Christianity is anything, it is brotherly kindness in all its living, active force; and if I have no more of the spirit of Christ than to let a brother stray off and off and off and finally be lost, then I have none at all of the spirit of Christ. Now, here we are, the churches in this town looking to see a gracious revival and thousands of souls turned to God. They would like to see millions of people brought to Christ. Well, brother, it is one thing to bring a soul to

Christ, and it is another thing to look after him after he gets there. Take an instance like this, happening in Rome, Ga. The pastor of the leading church in that city told me the incident. He said that a young man, perhaps twenty-two or twenty-three years old, was dying with consumption, and just the day before he died the young man said: "Brother L——, you are my pastor. I belong to your church. I joined your church three years ago, and I have tried to live right and do my duty; but," said he, "brother L——, not a single member of your church ever opened his mouth to me on the subject of religion. Not one came to me to speak a word of comfort or a word of cheer to me or a word of encouragement. And say to your church as you preach at my funeral, that, with 360 odd members, they have never been any help to me. And tell them, when I am dead and gone, never to do to any poor boy as they have done to me—just leave him to himself, and tell him to rough it." And I tell you to-day, from all the Christian churches in this country, men and women have strayed off, and made their way to hell that you never opened your mouth to on the subject of religion.

Oh, what a sad thought in human history! The brotherhood in Christ Jesus, the fatherhood of God, the brotherhood of the whole race. I declare to you to-day, there is nothing that I wouldn't do for my brother; there is nothing that I wouldn't sacrifice for my sister; there is no place at the table too good for my brother; there is no room in my house too good for my sister. And I say to you all that the brotherly kindness and the brotherly love that ought to be manifested one toward another have well-nigh died out from the face of the earth. Instead of helping each other and joining hands and marching like a band of brothers all through the world, there are members of different churches that don't know a dozen members of the same church they belong to. I have told them sometimes that I expect if they were to get to heaven—if they were fortunate enough to get there—the angels would be kept busy several years introducing them to one another.

If a Mason were to come here to St. Louis, and he needed assistance and needed help, and he was a Methodist as well as a Mason, which would he go to for help, the Methodist Church or the Masonic fraternity? If a man were an Odd Fellow and a Baptist, to which class would he go to get means to follow his journey? Would he go to the Odd Fellows or go to the Baptists? Ah, brother, the Irishman told a great truth when he said, "If there was a little more of the milk of human kindness in this world what a grand world would we have." I tell you, I had frequently rather go to a wholesale liquor dealer to get help than go to some members of the church.

And we can never accomplish what we ought to as a church unless this spirit of self-sacrifice, and of brotherly kindness and love shall take possession of us. [Here the speaker told of a lawyer, some fifty years of age, who joined the church of which he was pastor, in one of the wickedest counties in Georgia.]

And that man has never backslidden an inch in his life since he joined the church. An old brother at a camp-meeting once turned to me and said: "Jones, haven't you been a wonderful backslider in your day?" Said I: "I don't know. Why?" "Well," he says, "you seem to know more backsliders than I ever saw in my life." "Well," said I, "brother, I ought to begin to know something about them. I have never associated with any other sort since I joined the church." A fellow will learn something once in a while if he will keep eyes and ears open. Now, why was it this lawyer brother never backslid an inch? Do you want to know why? He literally spent his life in looking after backsliders. Shortly after he joined the church he commenced working with the brethren. If he saw two members of the church quarreling on the street, no matter what church they belonged to, he went out and put his hand on each's shoulder and said: "You are my brother. You are brethren to one another. You mustn't quarrel or fuss. If this is a question of financial difference I will pay the money out of my own pocket before I will see brothers fussing." And if a member of the church went into a grocery to get a drink he ran right in after him—not to take a drink with him, like some of you do, but to bring him out of there. And he walked into the grocery, and said he: "My brother, don't drink that, because Christian people ought not to drink. I used to drink when I was a child of the devil, but we can't drink whisky and be religious. My brother, walk out of here." And he would carry the brother out of there.

And if a member of the church got so drunk on the street that he could not walk home, he would say to another man, "Here is my brother drunk on the street, will you help to carry him down to the house with me? And he would carry that poor drunken fellow down to his house and say a word to his wife—the Major called his wife Sister Martha and Mary—and she was the best Martha I most ever saw, and she was the best Mary I think I ever saw. She was good on both sides. She would sit at the Saviour's feet and when she came to housekeeping everything about her home would shine—and he would say, "Sister Martha and Mary, here is one of our brothers slipped up; he's done a little wrong; fix a bed; let us put our brother to bed." And he woud be put to bed and the Major would sit by his side and say to his wife, "Fix a nice cup of coffee for our brother to drink when he wakes, and I'll pick out a few verses of Scripture to read to him, and I think he won't get drunk any more." And when he would wake up the Major would say to him, "Now, drink some of Sister Martha and Mary's coffee." And then he would show her the washstand and towel and invite her to wash the dirt off his face, and when he was straightened up he would kneel down by her and pray; "God help my brother. He has made a little slip, being tempted, but I don't think he'll do it any more." And he never had to take a man to his house but once. The first dose of that treatment generally fetched them.

A sister may say, "Ah, me! I would have no drunken dog in my bed!" That is because you are a good Sister Martha, but you are a failure as a Mary.

The Lord Jesus Christ lay out on that mountain top, bleak and dark and dreary, for forty days and forty nights, and suffered for you; the Lord Jesus Christ wept and prayed in the Garden of Gethsemane, with a bloody sweat bursting from His body, and expired on Calvary for you, and there you are, claiming to have the spirit of Christ, and you would not soil one of your snow-white counterpanes to save a soul from hell! Do you call that religion? Ah, me! We've got to be different if we ever do anything. We go to church and sing.

Christ gave his life for me,

And then we'll break out on the next line—

What have we done for him?

Just like we had done everything. And then we'll take up the next verse—

Christ suffered much for me,

59

And then we'll break out on the next line—

What have I suffered for him?

And there seems to be an exultation of soul as we strike that second line. Brother, sister, look at the life and character of Jesus Christ. Take the life and character of Paul! Take the life and character of those men who rotted to death in dungeons, and who died at the stake, and who were imprisoned and striped and abused for you and me, and then let us look how our hands have grown soft and white, and our own personal interest has absorbed all our energies and all our efforts.

I'll tell you where the rub is. There is a member of the church, and here is a poor drunkard; he walks up and gives his heart to God and joins the church, and that member of the church sits back there and shakes his head, "Oh, my soul! I wish that fellow hadn't joined our church"; and then, about three months after that, the poor fellow has tried to be faithful, but fell under temptation, and then the brother meets the preacher, and he tells him: "I knew you ought not to take that man into our church; I knew when he joined he would be disgracing our church." And I will tell you another thing: That poor fellow lying there in the gutter is a gentleman and a scholar and a Christian beside that old Pharisee, who stands by the side of him and says, "Just look at that! Just look at that!"

I will tell you, we got too much just such Phariseeism in this city as that. My God! help us to see that Jesus Christ died for the poorest and meanest wretch that ever walked on the face of the earth, and we can do nothing that can glorify Christ more than to put our arms around a poor, ruined wretch and bring him to God. And I praise my Saviour, now and forever, that He is able and willing, and seems more willing, to save the lowest, meanest man on earth than any other character that lives. That man may be so mean that the common people on the street kick him out of their way; the barrooms have kicked him out the door; his very wife has fled from him; but Christ says to all of us, when our father and mother forsake us, then He will takes us up. Oh, Christ! let the race of man be as good to each other as thou art good to us!

In the Fifth and Walnut Church at Louisville, Ky., two years ago, one night during a revival meeting, fifteen men came up and took the front seats, and those fifteen men on that front pew were the very imps of the devil. I never looked, and no man ever looked, at such men in a church of God. Now, how about those fifteen men? The pastor of that church—one of the sweetest-spirited, most Christly men I ever saw—he went to each one and took his name and said to him, "You remain here after this service." There sat the son of old Col. ———, who had been drunk on the streets of Louisville for twenty years; and here was another, the veriest reprobate that ever walked the face of the earth; and here was another, and there was another; and there the fifteen men sat, the very imps of the devil, at the very gates of hell, and that preacher took their names and asked them to remain. He took his board of stewards and said, after services: "Now, let us take these fifteen men to the bathroom, and let us take them to the clothing house and let us put clothes on them and have them made respectable and win them to Christ." And I was at that Louisville church just fifteen months after that. Now, how about the fifteen? One of them had died—had gone home to heaven; one of them had backslid, and thirteen of the most earnest workers at the Fifth and Walnut Church came off that front bench that I have been talking to you about, and the son of Col. ———, a bookkeeper for the Louisville and Nashville Railroad, and that same man would jump up in the meeting, now and then, and say: "Glory to God! I get up to say that God has saved the lowest sinner that lived in Louisville."

God help us to go out among the wharf rats and the degraded of this town and bring them to Christ. Poor fellows, how sorry we ought to be for them! They are kicked and cuffed about by humanity, and they toil every day for the meat they eat at night, and for the poor, cold house, and the shivering wife, and the ragged children. God help us to do what we can for those poor, degraded men! And when we see such a spirit as that among you all, then you may look for God to touch this city with a power that will move it from center to circumference.

Brethren, if a man be overtaken in a fault, ye which are spiritual go and restore him. It is not your business to criticize or say: "Just look how that man has degraded the church and disgraced Christianity," but it is your business to go out to him, and rescue him, and bring him back to God. There are many members of the church strayed off to-night and are wandering away from God that would have been good, active members of the church if you had been a brother, indeed, to them. "Brethren, if a man be overtaken in a fault, ye which are spiritual go and restore him." Why? If you don't you will backslide yourself. The spirit that makes you neglect your brother will make you backslide inevitably. Bishop Marvin, the noble man that died in your midst, related an incident how faithful class leaders cared for a poor drunken man and straightened him up, and brought him to God, and took him into the church, and labored with him, and labored for him, and had him praying night and morning in his family, and how that man moved out farther west, and how that man lived right there for several months, and how his wife wrote back to the noble class leaders and said to them: "My husband died happy last night and said, 'Write it back to my faithful class leaders there is another sinner saved by Christ.' "

Brethren, let us look to our Christianity. Does it send us out to those that need us? Is it bringing others to Christ through us? Are we spending and being spent year after year in the great work of seeing that souls are marching home to God?

Then I take this key and open it into another apartment of this chapter, and I read this: "Bear ye one another's burdens, and so fulfill the law of Christ."

I see in the Church of God that all of its duties rest on a few in all the churches. If you want any praying done, call on Brother A; if you want any paying done, call on Brother B, and all that sort of thing. And I want to tell you, we can never make the church what it ought to be until every man shall bear one another's burdens. We must do our part in all the phases of church work. I will tell how the thing stands now. You go about through the community and you will find the phases of church work. I will tell how the thing stands now. You go about through the community and you will find the whole of the church up in the wagon—the whole thing; some of them up there laughing, some dancing, some cursing, some shouting, some praying—the whole thing up in the wagon and the poor little preacher out in the shafts trying to pull the thing to glory, and every little while some fellow up in the wagon will say, "Tap him up a bit! Move him up a little, boys!" and feeding him on wheat straw all the year round. No horse ever made 2:40 on wheat straw.

Bear ye one another's burdens. Listen! If I were to go fishing to-morrow with four men, and we were to buy twenty-five cents' worth of lard to fry our fish, and we had to get wood to fry them, and prepare them to fry, if I didn't pay my five cents of that quarter, and I didn't get my part of the wood, and do my part of the cleaning of the fish, I would not consider myself a gentleman, much less a Christian. If I was a member of any church in this town, and I didn't do my part of the paying and my part of the praying and my part of the everything that was done, I wouldn't consider myself a gentleman, much less a Christian. The shirks and sharks in the church! And the shirk don't run long until he turns to the shark. He will shirk every day, and like the old shark he'll eat everything within a mile of him. There's a good deal of that sort going on in the world. And I will tell you where all the growling comes in. These fellows that don't pay any and don't pray any, they are the growlers, and there ought to be an addition to every church in this country, and call it "The Growler," and run them in there. If there is anything in the world I have got a contempt for it is to see two or three fellows sitting back in a Pullman sleeper with a dead-head ticket in their pockets quarreling with the conductor about how he is pulling the train.

Bear a part in the great work of bringing the world to God.

Then I take this same key and open into another apartment and read this: "For if a man think himself something, when he is [or when he does] nothing, he deceiveth himself."

What a man does is the test of what a man is. If what a man does is not a test of what a man is, then what a man pays is the test of what a man is. I can put up with a fellow

64

in the church that won't do anything, but who'll pay well. There ain't a railroad in heaven or earth that don't charge extra for a sleeper, and you ought to pay it. That's the truth about it. I believe in doing the thing yourself or hiring somebody else to do it. I will either pray every time they call on me at church, or I will have a fellow there paid by the month to do my praying—one or the other. And that's the only honest way to get out of it, sir. You've got a good many elements of the hog in you if you don't run it that way. I declare to you this shirking spirit—want all, all, all that can come to you and yet never give back anything—is too prevalent in the church to-day. And a man gets out of his religion just in proportion to what he puts into it. I used to be pastor; and I'll tell you another thing, I never had a member of my church in my life that would not pray in public and pray in his family, that was any account—never did.

What a man does is the test of what he is. If he runs on that line, there is the test. If he runs on this line, there is the test; and if a man thinks he must be doing something when he is doing nothing, he deceiveth himself. What an engine does is a test of what an engine is. When the president of the Wabash road writes to Mr. Rogers, at his locomotive works, and says: "I want an engine that will pull twenty cars up a grade of so many feet to the mile," Mr. Rogers sends an engine. They couple twenty cars to it and start it up the grade, but it stands stock still, and the president of the railroad telegraphs to Mr. Rogers: "Come after your engine; I don't want it." Mr. Rogers comes. They walk up to the engine and he says: "Look at that cab; it's the nicest cab ever sent out of the shop. Look at that bright piston rod how it glistens in the sunshine. Look at those magnificent driving wheels." The president replies, "I never said anything to you about cabs or piston rods or driving wheels. I want an engine that will take these cars up that grade." Another engine is built and it is ready for the trial. They fire her up until the gauge indicates 160 pounds pressure to the square inch. The engineer opens the throttle. The engine starts up hill, moving the cars with it, and when it turns the grade it seems to say, "I could have pulled up ten more cars if you had put them on the train." The president says, "That is what we want."

God does not want you because you live in a four-story house. He does not want you because you have the finest turnout in town. He does not want you because you are president of the leading bank. But God wants you for what you can do. Sister, God does not want you for how you can dress your children or how you can bang your hair. God wants you for what you can do.

There are some things you cannot delegate to another. I have a contempt for those folks who, when I go to their house, want me to conduct family prayers for them, and who never have any at any other time. Somehow, there is always something that will let the secret out. If a fellow is not in the habit of praying with his family you can always find it out without asking the question. An old preacher once went to a place like that. They asked him to read a chapter of the Bible and pray with them. After he had read a chapter of the Scriptures they all knelt down, and as they did so all the cats jumped out of the window. They had never seen anything like that before, and they did not know what was happening. I expect there is many a professing Christian in this house at whose home prayer is so great a stranger that if you were to pray with them the cats would jump out of the window. It is something unusual with them. I really believe some of us are like the man I once heard Dr. Young tell of. He awoke one morning and said to himself: "I have been a member of the church for fifteen years, and I have never been religious a single day." Afterward he lay there thinking and finally said, "I am going to put this day over as a Christian man. I am going to do my best this day to be religious." He got up out of his bed, and, kneeling down beside it, said, "Oh, Lord, help me to be a Christian this day. Help me this day to live aright." Then he rose from his knees, and before the breakfast bell rang he called his wife and family into the family room and said, "Take your seats. I'm going to read a chapter with you all. I have never lived religious one day in my life, but by God's grace I am going to put one day over religiously." Then he read a chapter of the Bible and offered up prayer. After breakfast he bade his wife and children good-by pleasantly. He was kind to all his clerks during the day, and gentle in all his transactions. He came back to dinner, and when he sat down he said grace—a "blessing," as we say—at his table. I like that, too. A man who will sit down to his table before his children and eat, without returning thanks to the Good Provider of all things, that fellow is eleven-tenths hog. All the human in him is turned to hog, and he is, at best, eleven-tenths hog. He sat down to his table and asked a blessing, and after dinner he said, "Wife, will you please fix up this half-broiled chicken here; make some nice toast, and will you arrange it nicely on a waiter for Brother Johnson, living down here. He has been paralyzed two years. He is a member of our church, and I have not been to see him. I have not paid any attention to him, but if you fix up these things nicely on a waiter I will take them down to him." The waiter was fixed up, and he took it down to the sick brother. Then he said: "If you have a Bible I will read to you," and he read: "The Lord is my shepherd. I shall not want." Then he knelt down and prayed heaven's blessing on the poor sick fellow. That night he held family prayer in his own home, and after they had gone to bed, his sons Bill and Tom, who slept in the next room, with the door open between, began talking. Tom hunched Bill in the side and said: "Bill, the old man's going to die"; and Bill said: "How do you know, Tom?" "Why," said Tom, "don't you see he is getting pious?"

Let me tell you, there is many a Christian in this town whose children, if he were to go home and resolve to be religious for one day, would punch one another in the short ribs and say, "The old man is going to die."

And now let us go away and think about the part we are to take in this great work. "How am I to prepare myself, and what shall I do, in order that God may carry on and bless this work?" And now, brethren, Christian brethren of all churches, if you have it in your hearts will you stand squarely on your feet and say, "God helping me, I intend to live an unselfish Christian. I intend to try to be a good man and to help others to be good"? Will everybody of every church that feels that way stand up? Well, thank God for such a house as that, and may God inspire you to lead a better life. And may the blessing of Almighty God abide with you for ever and ever. Amen.

Many a man imagines he has religion when he only has a liver complaint.

S. J.

4. EVERYDAY RELIGION

WE INVITE YOUR ATTENTION TO THE TEXT, TO BE FOUND IN the third chapter and ninth verse of the first epistle general of St. John.

Whosoever is born of God doth not commit sin; for his seed remaineth in him; and he cannot sin, because he is born of God.

You say, "Strange text for a Thanksgiving sermon." Well, let's wait awhile and see what this text has to do with this occasion and with the future of our lives. I might stop here and say: "This one verse of Scripture gave me more pain and trouble for seven or eight years of my religious life than perhaps any other and all other passages of the word of God. This text to me once was a two-edged sword, and I never approached it that I didn't feel its sharp blades cutting asunder the very joint and marrow and soul and spirit." To a great many, the reading of this text is nothing more than the applying of the sound, but to others and to me, while this text was once a two-edged sword, now it is the sweetest bread heaven ever gave me. I announce at this point that I don't propose to preach on sanctification. I don't expect to touch any controversial point, any controversial dogmas and views. I am going to preach an old-fashioned righteousness and the life of the really converted man. I'm going to preach on everyday religion. I shall not get up as high as sanctification, though I believe in it with all my heart, and I believe that without holiness no man shall see the Lord, and if you ask me why I believe that, I tell you just because the Bible says so, and I don't want any better reason for anything than that "God says."

Now, this text is the climax of that preceding, and we can only reach this great climactical point as we may come up through the context. And may God help me to preach this text. I would rather partially fail on this text than succeed on many other texts on the word of God. A clear exegesis, a scriptural understanding of this text to-day, must benefit every man here, and every woman here, whether you profess to be Christians or not. And now I turn to the context, beginning with the first verse, and I read this:

> Behold, what manner of love the Father hath bestowed upon us, that we should be called the sons of God: therefore the world knoweth us not because it knew him not. Beloved, now are we the sons of God and it doth not yet appear . . .

The first announcement of the text is the princely character of the Christian man: "Now are we the sons of God."

What a blessed realization this is to poor, weak humanity. And thank God! The sentiment of the song is but the truth of God's words when we sing:

> I'm a child of the King,
> My father is rich in houses and lands.

Every Christian man must realize, first, I am a son of the Lord God Almighty. He is my father. I am His child. It is worth a great deal to a man, brother, to know and be conscious of the fact that he belongs to a noble family. It is worth a great deal to any man to know that the blood which courses through his veins is as pure and good as ever flowed through human veins. It is worth a good deal to a boy to know that his father was a princely good man. It is worth a great deal to a boy to look back with the consciousness, "My mother was one of the purest women that ever lived." In fact, many a boy has drifted to the very verge of destruction in his waywardness and dissipation, and in some thoughtful moment a kind friend has approached him and laid his hand on his shoulder and said: "My friend! Young man! Why will you dissipate and why will you go so far in sin? My precious young man, your mother was one of the most princely women I ever knew. Your father was a noble Christian man." And the boy has walked off alone and buried his face in his hands and wept like a child as he said: "My mother was one of the purest women earth ever knew. My father was a noble, princely man. And to-day I reform my life and serve my mother's God and follow my father's Christ."

I once knew a man in Mississippi; he was an elegant man, some fifty years old, an elegant, cultured gentleman. He was what we call an agnostic, or infidel. After the meeting had progressed several days, he stood up one morning in the vast congregation and he said: "My fellow citizens, I have roamed over all the range of science and literature. I have never found rest to my soul, and to-day my mind turns back to the purest, sweetest mother a boy ever had. My mind goes back to my precious father and the family altar and the sacred conversations at home, and I stand up to-day to confess my sins and give my life to Christ."

Ah, me! if we realize who we are, then that will help us to be what we ought to be.

A certain one of the crowned heads of an Eastern country turned his son over to a tutor to train and educate. He was an unruly boy, some twelve years of age, and the great question of the tutor was: "How will I manage this boy? I cannot use a rod on the king's son. How am I to manage him?" And, finally, he adopted this plan: He made a bow of ribbon and bound it on the lapel of the boy's coat. The boy turned to the tutor and said: "What does that mean?" The tutor said: "That is the sign of your royal character. That is the sign that you are the son of a king. That is the emblem of your royal character." And ever after that, when the boy misbehaved the teacher pointed his finger to the badge, and the boy subsided in a moment and begged pardon for his rudeness. And St. Paul says: "I carry about with me the marks of the Lord Jesus Christ, and when the good spirit of Christ drops his finger on the mark I stop all that is evil and weep my life away for having grieved God's love."

[Here Mr. Jones referred to the visit of Prince Edward of England to this country, to the wish expressed that while here he would behave himself as became his rank, and to the general verdict of approval of his conduct while in America, and said:]

Now, I may not and cannot announce that I am the son of Queen Victoria of England, but, blessed be God! I am the son of Lord God Almighty, and I am heir apparent to all things. And when I walk out before the world, and make the declaration, the world greets me, and replies: "Now we expect something of you. We want you to talk like a prince, to give like a prince, to act as a prince, to go where princes ought to go, and stay away from where princes ought not to go. We want you to behave as a worthy member of the family to which you belong," and, brethren, the highest aim of a Christian's heart is to worthily magnify the name of the family to which he belongs, and, oh, how it ought to be the chief desire of all Christian hearts never to bring reproach or shame on the name of the family of God.

One of the purest of men, your noble bishop, who died in your midst, in one of his sermons, said this: "Shortly after I joined the church, I was riding along, when this thought impressed me: 'I am now a member of the Church of Christ, and I have it in my power to bring reproach and shame on the name and cause of Christ.' " Said he, "When that thought possessed me, it overwhelmed me. Oh, what a fearful power delegated to mortal man! Power to bring reproach and shame on the cause of Christ. And the prayer that I lifted up from my heart, was, 'God help me to die rather than bring a stain on the family of God and the name of Christ.' "

When you walk out before the world with this announcement made: "I am the child of the King, I am heir apparent to all things," the world doffs its hat, and says to you: "We expect you to live like one," and I am very glad this world will not compromise Christian people down to the point where they will willingly let us do like they do. I am glad that no wicked man ever sees a professing Christian doing anything wrong that he doesn't point the finger of scorn at him, and say: "Just look at that professing Christian. He dishonors his God, and digraces himself." I say I am glad the world thinks more of Christ, and thinks more of Christianity, than to let us Christian people misrepresent the Gospel, and misrepresent Christ, without throwing it in our teeth, and telling us to our face: "We believe you are hypocrites." I am glad of that.

And then, after a profession like this, it behooves us to be grateful for the redeeming mercy and condescending grace that would adopt us into the heavenly family. It behooves us then to lead a pure life and stainless character before God and men.

Now are we the sons of God—It isn't by and by. It isn't when I am bidding earth and friends good-by, and pluming myself for flight to glory and God, but it is down in the world of temptation and trial. Every morning, noon and night, I may fall on my knees and say, "My Father, which art in heaven." I can explain my existence on no other hypothesis than that God is my Father.

I was getting on a railroad train some months ago in my State, and a gentleman boarded the train at one of the stations, and after shaking hands and talking a moment I asked him the news. "Well," he said, "nothing special I believe, except I came very near being killed last night." Said I, "How was that?" Said he, "The agent at the depot in our town was lying on the platform of the depot, drunk. He had been drunk several days. I went up to him to help him into the depot, and when I did so he jerked out his pistol and shot at me twice, and came very near hitting me." "Well," said I, "do you mean to say that the agent at the depot in your town had been drunk for several days? Why, the officers of this road are very strict with their employes. How is it this man maintains his position if he drinks that way?" Said the gentleman, "I can't tell you, sir, only this man, this agent, is brother-in-law to the president of the road." Well, when he said that, I saw it all in a moment, and then I said to myself: "How is it God puts up with me as He does? How is it God has borne with me as He has?" And I found the answer is this: Not because God was my brother-in-law, but because God was my Father; and isn't it astonishing how God will bear with His children?

I learned a great lesson in my relations toward God in a little incident that happened at my own home. We had in our employ a colored servant girl nursing for us. She was rather a careless, indifferent servant. I was sitting in the room one morning just after breakfast, and this girl walked in and my wife said: "Sally, you can go to your home this morning, and tell your mother to come over after a while and I will pay your wages to her. I don't want you any longer, Sally; you may go." I looked up from my book, and the girl stood there, full face toward my wife, and the tears commenced running down her cheeks, and directly she turned to my wife and she said: "Mrs. Jones, please, ma'am, don't turn me off. I know I'm the poorest servant you ever had, but I don't want to be turned off. Please, ma'am, keep me." I commenced to beg for the poor girl, and said: "Wife, bear with her a little while longer." And then I thought to myself: "If the Lord Jesus were to come down this morning and discharge me and tell me, 'I don't want you any longer,' I would fall down at His feet and say: 'Blessed Saviour, don't turn me off. I know I am the poorest servant you ever had, but, blessed Christ, keep me in thy life employ.'"

Oh, blessed Christ! So good to us! So merciful to us! Ah, brother,

> When all thy mercies, oh, my Lord,
>   My rising soul surveys,
> Transported by the view, I'm lost
>   In wonder, love and praise.
>
> Oh, after love like this,
>   Let rocks and hills their silence break,
> And all harmonious human tongues
>   Their Saviour's praises speak.

"Herein is love; not that we loved him, but that he loved us and gave his own Son to die for us."

"God so loved the world that he gave his only begotten Son," that every child of heaven might be adopted into the heavenly family and become an heir of immortal life. Ah, look up to-day, and see your father's face as it shines in beauty and love and mercy, and say: "Abba, Father, my Lord and my God!" And then realizing your princely character ever after this,

> Let your life and lips express
> The holy Gospel you profess.

And then I turn to the second feature of the text, and I read it this way:

Now are we the sons of God, and it doth not yet appear what we shall be; but we know that when he shall appear, we shall be like him, for we shall see him as he is. And he that hath this hope in him purifieth himself even as Christ is pure.

The Christian character is pure. There is a great deal said about life purity and heart purity in the Word of God. The Christian is pure in his life and pure in his character. The Book says: "Blessed is the man unto whom the Lord imputeth not iniquity, and in whose spirit there is no guile."

A guileless man! A guileless woman! A guileless husband! A guileless wife! A guileless child! A purity like the character of the little ermine, that beautiful, fastidious little animal, with its hair and skin almost as white as the driven snow, and the only way to capture it, with its cunning, is to mark its course from its home, and then sprinkle mud and dirt along its pathway, and when the little ermine reaches in its pathway to where the muddy

water and dirt are placed, it will lie down and subject itself to capture and death before it will smirch or soil one
of its snow-white hairs. And so the true Christian has
reached his highest aims when he reaches a point where
he will lie down and subject himself to torture and death
before he will smirch his character as a Christian man.
That's the Christian character—princely in nature and
pure in character.

Brethren, sooner or later, we must meet this point, that
God's people are a peculiar people and God's people are
a pure people. Sooner or later, we must meet this in our
convictions, in our intelligent thought; and I say to you
all that there is no theological book in any theological
library in the country, Protestant in its character, that
puts salvation this side of these three principles. Salvation,
says all Protestant theology, is deliverance from the guilt
of sin, deliverance from the love of sin, and deliverance
from the dominion of sin. And I declare to you to-day that
the Gospel of Jesus Christ is either adequate to reach the
depths of human depravity, or we misunderstand that Gospel.

I am ready to take this position and defy earth and hell
equally upon it. Jesus is able to do for me and you all that
we need to have done, and if that is true, then God knows
I need to be delivered from sin, its dominion, its love and
its guilt. Now, when I am delivered from the guilt of sin,
I have got to that point in the Christian life reached by
Bunyan's pilgrim when he walks to the cross, and the burden rolls from his conscience, and he stands upright before
God. But, brother, that is not sufficient. The mere pardoning power that would leave me as I was doesn't amount to
much. I not only want to be pardoned for my past sins, but
I want to be cleansed from all unrighteousness.

In every thought renewed,
   And full of life divine,
Perfect and right and pure and good,
   Lord keep me ever thine.

If I had but one prayer between this and eternity, I would pour out my soul in this one petition: "God, give me a pure heart and a pure life—the purity of Christian character."

I don't consider any man safe here or hereafter until he is delivered from the love of those things that are wrong. There is no attitude toward God that is acceptable to Him, except the attitude that turns with loathing away from sin. Let me illustrate what I mean: Here's a mother sitting quietly within her room. Her only child, little Willie, just four years old, the pride of her heart and the joy of her life, sees mamma's little pearl-handled pen knife lying on the table. That little knife is the present of a friend, and mother values it highly. Little Willie, unknown to mother, picks up the little knife and runs out of the room, and in an hour mother wonders where he is, and directly the nurse comes in hurriedly and says: "Little Willie is lying all bloody in the front flower yard," and mother rushes out there, and there is little Willie just gasping and breathing his last. He stubbed his little foot and fell and the blade pierced the jugular vein. The mother grabs the little bloody angel in her arms and runs into the room and just as she lays him on the little bed he breathes his last, and the mother kisses her child and says: "Sweet Willie, just speak one more time." Next day, mother carries little Willie to the grave and buries him, and comes back to her home with broken heart, and as she sits down and turns back the dark veil, the nurse comes out of the front yard and says: "Madam, here's the little knife. Here's your little pearl-handled knife." The mother looks at the knife and its blade all covered with the blood of her sweet child, and she shrinks back in horror and says, "Take that knife out of my presence. I never want to see it again. It has the blood of my precious child on it." And when a Christian man or woman, under the light of God's Holy Spirit, can see that every sin in all the moral universe of God has been covered with the blood of the Son of God, then he shrinks back in horror and says: "Oh, take it out of my presence! It is covered with the precious blood of my bleeding Saviour." Oh, brother, you will never know what piety is until you see all impurity bathed in the blood of the Son of God. Oh, let us hate sin and abhor it, and turn away from it and despise it utterly.

He that is born of God doth not commit sin, for his seed remaineth in him and he cannot sin because he is born of God. We have had, first, the princely character of the Christian, and, second, his purity of character, and now we come to the climax of the text, the imperviousness of the Christian character to sin.

Now, if I were to say right here that an honest man cannot steal, everybody would say, "That is true." If I were to say a sober man cannot get drunk, they would say, "That's a fact." If I were to say a chaste man cannot be vulgar, they would say, "That is true." Well, now, brother, if a truthful man as a truthful man cannot tell a lie, and an honest man as an honest man cannot steal, and a sober man as a sober man cannot get drunk—if logic is worth anything and common sense and religion will mix up together at all, then I say, Is there anything unreasonable in the proposition that "he that is born of God doth not commit sin"?

Don't you see? "He that is born of God doth not commit sin, because his seed remaineth in him."

Now, there's the gist of the whole matter. There's the pivotal point in the whole text: "because his seed remaineth in him."

It is a moral "can't," not a physical "can't." Now, suppose some man had said to me this morning when I got up, "Brother Tudor came here last night and stole your watch and clothes, and has run away." I would look the man in the face and say, "Brother Tudor cannot steal my watch and clothes." I don't mean that he could not have walked out on the street and gone into my room and carried off these things as a physical act, but I say, "It is against his principle and against his interest and against his conviction and against his desires and purposes and everything, and I just know he didn't do it."

There's a man with the love and respect of everybody in St. Louis, and with no interest at all for stealing anything from me, and I just know he couldn't do it; and if every man in the city of St. Louis was like him, we could quit shutting our front doors at night and throw all our keys away, and just close up our sheriff's institution and every jail and calaboose in this city. It is like a train when you see it going thundering along the track toward Kansas City, you know it isn't going to St. Louis because all its momentum is the other way. And when a man's momentum and desires and purposes and intentions are set heavenward, with all the power that God can give him, then he can't go to hell.

Now, you know that line you sing:

> Surely the Captain may depend on me.

How few of us the Lord can depend on, and how few can He trust with money! You hear men confessing every sin except that of avarice. I never heard of anything of that sort in the church, never. There are men in this town, and, I expect, some men in this house, that if God were to check on you to-day for $100 or $1,000 for some good cause, you would let that check go to protest, and swear you didn't have the money. And yet if you could go down here on a certain corner and buy a piece of property at thirty-three per cent discount, you would give a cash check for every dollar of it. And God keeps books and He'll put your sort in hell by and by for lying, if you never do anything else wrong.

The idea of the divine spirit taking possession of our hearts means about this: My time and life and hands and feet and tongue all belong to God. I never intend to work for the devil. I have no time. Here's a fellow who goes over to one of these ladies and says: "Can you go to the theater with me to-night?"

"No."

"Why not?"

"Well, this is my night for visiting the sick."

"Will you go to-morrow night?"

"No."

"Why?"

"Because to-morrow night is our Bible lesson night, when myself and children study the lesson for Sunday."

"How about the night after that?"

"I can't go that night either. That's prayer-meeting night, and I never miss prayer meeting."

"Will you go the next night?"

"That's the night we meet at the church parlor to study the Sunday-school lesson."

"Well, now, when will you go?"

"I don't know any night I can give you in the next thousand years. I might fix up one a thousand years from now, but I haven't any night in a thousand years that I can give for that."

Don't you see? That lady has got where she's worth something to God and worth nothing to the devil.

Oh, Lord, give us that sort of religion all over this country. Amen.

We are all created on a common platform; we are all redeemed on a common platform. When God gave one a chance He threw the gates open to all.

S. J.

5. WALKING WITH CHRIST

WE INVITE YOUR ATTENTION TO THREE WORDS TO BE FOUND in the first verse of the eighth chapter of St. Paul's Epistle to the Romans:

There is therefore now no condemnation to them which are in Christ Jesus.

These are the three words: "In Christ Jesus—who walk not after the flesh, but after the spirit."

The law, said Blackstone, is a rule of action prescribed by the supreme power of the State, commanding what is right and prohibiting what is wrong. The law is a rule; the law is a line; the law is a straight edge. And the law of God may map out, and does map out, a rule of action, but has nothing in itself to give me an inspiration that would incline me to walk on it and to walk straightly by it. The law of God in this sense is a mirror and simply a mirror. A mirror placed before my form would reveal any defects of my face, any mud or smut, and I might see plainly the defects and I might plainly see the mud and smut, but if I wanted to wash it off I could not wash it off with a mirror. The mirror would simply show me it is there, and has no power to remove it. The law of God reveals my defects. It shows me how crooked I am, without any power in the world to straighten me. And the man who sees right, the man who admits that the rule is right and straight, and at the same time has no inspiration, no power within him, no help within him to keep him on this straight line, realizes just what Paul did when he said: "Oh, wretched man that I am! Who will deliver me from this body of death?"

Who will take and loose from me this dead body that is chained to me and carry it away from me? The memories of my imperfections, my frailties, my shortcomings, are like a body of death chained to me. They are a weight of guilt. And the offensive odors of past sins are indeed like a dead body chained to a man. Now, our Saviour lifts the curtain. The book lifts the curtain. Further along it tells us, "Christ is the end of the law for righteousness to every one that believeth."

It tells us again that with faith unfeigned and a pure conscience we may know what it is to be "in Christ Jesus a new creature."

Now, understand that depravity I never discuss at all, as to whether it is partial or total; whether it is simply innate or developed. We say nothing about it. But I meet every man on the face of this earth, and look him in the eye and tell him: "Naturally, innately, you have meanness enough in you to damn you, and I don't know what a fellow wants with any more than that." He is greedier than I have ever been if he wants any more than that. Whether it is partial or total, I have no capacity, may be, and, I am satisfied, no time or inclination, to discuss. Now, before us we have a straight line, and we all admit we cannot walk on it, and heaven is just at the other end of that straight line for every one of us. Now, some people propose to dodge and shirk and beat around and come out all right. Well, now, if you can tell me how a man can take a short cut on a straight road, then I'll be able to tell something about how a fellow can whip round and jerk round and come out even at the end. I could sort of understand it then. But straight is the gate, and straight is the line, and straight is the way, and there are no right cuts on a straight road that I know anything about.

And St. Paul reaches the conclusion that I wish we would all reach. This seventh chapter of Romans is full of mystery, and I think with the preacher who said that if we had gotten out of the seventh chapter of Romans into the eighth the devil would get us all. I think that he was about right. And now we come to the first verse of the eighth chapter: "There is therefore now no condemnation to them which are in Christ Jesus."

"In Christ Jesus." Being "in Christ Jesus" and having "Christ in you" are interchangeable terms in Scripture.

"Having Christ in you, form the hope of glory," is one way to put it. Another is: "If any man be in Christ Jesus he is a new creature."

Our Saviour amplified the thought when He said: "Behold I stand at the door and knock. If you will open unto me I will come in and sup with you."

Oh, blessed thought! Christ my guest! I am ashamed of what I have to offer Him. I am ashamed of the table I set Him down to. I am ashamed of everything in the home I invite Him to. But He sits there, and He is my guest but a moment until He stands up and says: "Now you be my guest and I will be host." Oh, what a privilege to sit at a table with Christ as host, and have Him feed us on heaven's bread and angels' food.

In Christ Jesus. If you be in Christ Jesus you are a new creature, if He form in you the hope of glory. I want to say that it is peculiarly true of Christianity that we need a Christ. Not a Christ of history, not a Christ of eighteen hundred years ago, not a Christ on Calvary, but a present, abiding Christ. You can run Mormonism with Joe Smith and Brigham Young in their graves; it goes right on. You can run Confucianism without Confucius. But you can't run Christianity without Christ. This Christianity is the personal living embodiment of Christ. And the question comes up there, and it is the question of this nineteenth century: Who is Christ? What is Christ? Do you know there have been more lives of Christ written since I was born than were ever written before I was born. In the last thirty-eight years there have been written more lives of Christ than in all the past ages since He walked among men. Isn't that a singular fact! Isn't it carrying out the thought expressed by him: "And I, if I be lifted up, will draw all things unto me"?

Who is Christ? What is Christ? This world has always been eager to know and eager to see. Thousands of years ago, when the people of this old world groped in darkness and mingled as orphans at one tomb, they grew restless and turned their eyes up to the darkened heavens and bent their ears upward, and almost in the language of despair they said, "Oh, tell us who thou art, thou great infinite one. Are we here simply by accident, or is there a great first cause? Tell us who thou art." And as they eagerly listened a voice issued out from the darkness—a still, small voice—and answered back, "I am." They caught it up and repeated it—"I am." They said, "Here is some light, but, oh, how dark it is!"

And the world groped on in darkness for centuries, and by and by, restless and nervous and impatient, they turned their faces back up to heaven and bent their ears and cried again, "Oh, tell us who thou art, what thou art to us!" And the voice answered back: "I am what I am. I am that I

90

am." And they caught it up and said: " 'I am that I am. Here's a little more light. We are thankful for any light. Oh, how dark it is!"

And by and by the earth grew restless and rushed right up on One who was speaking, and they said: "Be quiet. Let us see what He says." And He answered and said: "I am"—and they caught it up, "I am." We have heard that before. Listen, we will get a light now. "I am." Everything and everybody be quiet. Let us hear Him speak. He said: "I am the way." Oh, ye lost men that have been wandering in the wilderness for hundreds of years, hear Him speak! Here's a thoroughfare, a highway, a road we may walk in. Oh, ye lost men of earth, come into this way and rejoice that you are in a highway.

Listen! He is going to speak again: "I am the truth." Oh, this old world has been wrapped in error thousands of years, and now we are seeing the truth. We have not seen the truth for thousands of years. And now let us listen; we have the truth from Him who is the very embodiment of truth: "I am the truth."

Listen! He speaks again: "I am the bread." Oh, listen, ye hungry souls! Here's bread enough and to spare. Come and eat and be satisfied.

Listen! He is speaking again: "I am the water." Oh, ye thirsty men that have been famishing in the desert of life, listen! Here's the living fountain and ye may drink and never be thirsty any more.

Listen! He speaks again: "I am the door." And "door" means house and home, and hospitality and comfort. Oh, ye poor wandering houseless men, listen! Here is home for all the children of men.

Listen! He speaks again: "I am the light." You old world, that has groped in darkness, wake up under this golden light and let them see just as God would have them see!

In Christ Jesus. Do you recollect the occasion when the apostles went to the Master and said: "Master, a great multitude has been following us now for days, and they have famished for hunger! Master, bid them go away and get something to eat." Jesus looked at His disciples—you recollect—and He said a thing world-wide in its meaning, and that has given me comfort in the darkest hours of my religious life—do you recollect what Jesus said? "They need not depart. They needn't go away from me for anything. You get out your little loaves and fishes and I will multiply them until this multitude shall be fed and until they shall realize that around Christ centers all, and that he is all and in all." Blessed be God! A man need not go away from Christ to get anything that is necessary for him in time or necessary for him in eternity.

Now, with such a one before you, I want to say the question comes up, "Who is Christ?" at last. What is Christ? That is the question. Our finest authors have written and I have been charmed with Beattie and with Farrar and with Young and with our best authors on this subject, but, brothers, do you know that one of the disciples wrote the history of Christ in a single line—I believe in five words: "He went about doing good"?

Well, now, when we bring this problem down to where we can get hold of it, we see that Jesus Christ was the living, personal, embodiment of wisdom, and justice and love and mercy and truth and of all the characteristics that make God lovely. That is it. And if my salvation or your salvation depended on our picking a single flaw in the life of Christ, or picking out a single utterance of His that was below the dignity of God, we would essentially and inevitably be damned forever, for after all infidelity has said, it cannot pick a flaw in His life nor find an utterance that was below the dignity of a God.

What is Christ? The living personal embodiment of wisdom and justice and truth and love and mercy and forgiveness and all those attributes that make the character of God lovely. That's it.

Well, now, how may a man determine whether he has Christ or not? If he be in Christ Jesus, then he is a wise man and a just man and a true man and a forgiving man and a lovely character. Don't you see? St. Paul said: "I am crucified with Christ; yet, nevertheless, I live. Yet not I, but Christ liveth in me."

That is, "Christ propels these hands and feet and tongue just as he did his own hands and feet and tongue."

I die daily. There is the secret of a Christian's happy life. And by that St. Paul meant this: "The first thing I do in the morning when I open my eyes is to fall down on my knees and die to this world; die to its pleasures, its profits, its fruits, its smiles, its condemnations; die to its threats; die to its money; die to all it can do." And when Paul got up from his knees in the morning he was as dead to this world as he was afterwards when his head was severed from his body and his body buried out of the sight of men. And a man never truly lives until he dies in this sense, and when a man dies in this sense he is the livest man that ever walked on the face of the earth.

A Christian must essentially be a wise man. What is wisdom? It is the skillful application of knowledge. It is using what I have at command to the best end in the best way. That's it. Wisdom! Wisdom! There are a great many knowing men in this world, but very few wise men. We have knowledge enough to run about four such worlds as this, but haven't wisdom enough to keep out of jail a large class of society, and a larger other class, perhaps, ought to be there.

Wisdom—sense enough, and the right use of sense enough, to do the best thing and do it in the best way. Well, now, what is the wisdom of Christianity? I tell you it is the use of the best means to the best ends. And I tell you how I look at it. I have been listening ever since I was converted, and I want to say right here, on this point, that I never heard a man tell his experience, and state in his experience some Christian duty that helped him to be religious, that I didn't adopt that myself. I just think, "Well, old fellow, if that helped you, I think it will help me. I have started in in cold-blooded earnest to get to the good world, and I'll adopt anything that will help me along. That's my program." When I heard an old Christian say: "Family prayer was a great blessing," thinks I to myself, "God helping me, I'll adopt it. I want everything that will help me to get on, and I want to adopt every plank in the platform that ever helped a man to be good, and ever helped a man to overcome sin and wickedness. These little, slow Christians in this land, they have just got two planks in their religious platform. Saying a little prayer, and reading a little Bible, is just as far as they ever get. That is all there is in their religion—saying a prayer every night before they go to bed, and reading the Bible a little occasionally. I tell you they sometimes remind me of these little two-wheeled engines they made when they first started to make engines. They just put two wheels under them and they made schedule time, three miles an hour, right along.

But people got tired of that sort of schedule. Wisdom says, "That won't do—three miles an hour for a locomotive engine!" Well, now what do they do? They just put jack-screws under that engine and prized it up, and put six more wheels beneath her. That's all; and now you can go fifty or sixty or even seventy-nine miles an hour. What do you say to that? That is a good schedule. And now, brother, sister, God help you to be willing, anxious for God Almighty to prize you up and put more wheels under you. These little two-wheeled fellows, they start out toward the good world and have been running the Christian race for forty years, and haven't gotten ten miles on their journey. The devil can take one of these little two-wheeled fellows and give him ten miles' start, and then catch him before breakfast every time. That's the plain truth about it.

Oh, sir, wisdom says to me: "Be prized up closer to God, and let every Christian duty be a wheel put in, and then you will roll on to God successfully, and can outrun the devil in any race he wants to make with you. You move faster and you move more grandly.

Wisdom! Do the right thing and do it in the right way. Adopt every plank in your religious platform that ever helped a man to be good, and tear out every one that ever helped a man to be bad. Wisdom! Justice! Ah, justice! I have heard people say, "Christ was a just man." I have heard people say, "You had better be just than generous." Did you know that it is ten times as hard to be just as to be generous? Almost any man can pull out a ten dollar bill and give it to a widow. That is generosity. But it takes a man—a true man—that will sit down and draw the line and give to God His dues, to his neighbors their dues, to his family their dues, and to the world its dues. It is very hard to find a generous man in this world, and it is ten thousand times harder to be just than generous. I like a man to be just to his family, just to his God, just to humanity. A man that will be just in his relative duties to humanity and to himself. A just man weighs everything in the balance. Ah, me! Burns told the truth when he said:

> Ouch! Mankind are but unco' weak
> And little to be trusted.
> When self the wavering balance shakes,
> It's rarely right adjusted.

There are a great many preachers in this world—I may be one of them—I am no better than any of them—that have a great many converts every year, and they say, "I've had two hundred conversions." Well, converted from what and converted to what?" That's the question! And when you ring the changes on the preacher right there, and say: "Brother, you say you got two hundred converts?" "Yes." "Well, what have they been converted from, and what have they been converted to?" Now, if you can find me a man that has been converted from the works of the flesh, which are manifest—idolatry, witchcraft, hatred, malice, riot, strife, sedition, heresy, licentiousness, and all that sort of thing—he is converted over to love and mercy and justice and wisdom, and all these other things that God approves of, then, I say, you get a fellow who is converted on the Bible platform, and I would not give a flip of my finger for a man converted on any other platform. Two hundred converts! A fellow out in the country gets up a big meeting and he has two hundred converts. Does he mean he has two hundred more like those he got before —those quarter-of-a-dollar and ten-cents-a-year admission fellows and a demijohn sitting around in every house? Does he mean that he has got two hundred more like that?

Converted from what and converted to what? Christianity is not a song or a sentiment, or a shout or a joining the church, but is a great principle, buoying up itself and manifest. It is wisdom and love and mercy and justice, and every good word and work—that is it.

Well, to be practical all through—being in Christ Jesus presupposes, first, a longing desire for Christ, a longing desire for the true and the noble and the good and the just. Oh, me, brother, is there a man here who down in his heart never had a longing desire for a better life and a nobler life and a truer life? Is there one? Is there a man here that never wished down in his soul he was a wiser man, a more just man, a more loving man, and a more forgiving man?

Brother, you know what the Scripture says is a healthy, good condition? Spiritual hungering and thirsting after righteousness. That is a healthful religious experience—hungering and thirsting after righteousness. Oh, brother, being in Christ Jesus presupposes a longing for Christ, a desire for Christ. That's it. David said: "My heart panteth after the living God as the heart panteth for the water brook."

Longing for Christ, hungering, thirsting after righteousness. The supremest passion of a man's life is his hunger and his thirst. Did you ever locate the sensation of physical hunger—did you ever locate it? The little fellow struck it right. When you are next intensely hungry you locate the sensation and it is just at this point (indicating under the right eye), and the little fellow said, "Pa, I'm hungry," and his father said, "Son, how do you feel when you feel hungry?" He said, "I feel like I want to chaw something." Now, the little fellow had it rightly. The sensation of physical hunger is located right here, but the sensation of spiritual hunger is located in the will, it is located in the affections, it is located in the inner man. I long for something better and nobler and truer and grander. I long for Him

97

who was the embodiment of all that was true and all that was good. That's it. Longing for Christ! The soul never reaches Him until nothing but Christ will satisfy the soul.

I have seen the little two-year-old boy. The nurse has him in her arms and he is wringing and twisting and crying. His mother is out; his mother is gone to town; his mother, is shopping; and little Willie twists and cries and kicks and slips; and away he goes, and the nurse gets his toys. "I don't want no toys," and she gets his marbles. "I don't want no marbles," and she gets him some candy. "I don't want no candy, I don't want no candy; I want mama; I don't want those marbles; I want mama; I don't want those playthings; I want mama." And presently mama steps in the door and the little fellow is satisfied and he runs up to her and throws his arms around her neck and he is as sweet as a little angel. Mama has come. That's what he wanted. And I like to see a Christian whose soul longs for Christ, who won't be satisfied with anything else. "Here is a ball." "I don't want any ball." "Here is a theater." "I don't want any theater." "Here is money." "I don't want any money; I don't want anything; I want Christ and I won't have anything else," and he won't want anything else. And Christ always comes to the soul that will have nothing but Him, and He never comes to a soul while anything else would satisfy it. A fellow says: "I sought religion a whole month and I never got it." You got something else. That is what satisfied you. And Christ never comes to the soul until the soul reaches the point where nothing will satisfy but Him.

Sister, this last cruel war—some wives present may know what I am talking about—this last cruel, bloody war—how husband kissed you good-by in the early part of '61, and went to the cruel war, and how you watched every mail and all the telegraphic reports, and how anxiously you looked to the battlefield, until, by and by, husband is gone two months, six months, ten months, twelve months, twenty months, thirty months. The sole desire of the wife's heart and soul was for her husband to return, and nothing would satisfy or gratify the longing, loving wife but the presence of her husband; and, oh! how she looked, and how she longed and waited, and how all other pleasures and all other enjoyments faded away in her presence, in the presence of this one intense, eternal longing of her soul for husband's return.

Take the case of Penelope, perhaps the most beautiful woman in the world's history. When Ulysses went to the war, and after several months and two years all tidings of him were lost, and this beautiful woman had other suitors, and they pressed her hand, she waited to hear from him she loved, and they pressed her hand, for years they pressed her hand, and, at last, her suitors were so eager that she finally said: "Gentlemen, if you will wait until I weave out this piece of cloth in the loom, then I will give you an answer." And then she sat and wove all day and unraveled it all night, and thus she worked and toiled, and for ten more long years in her weary weaving she kept the suitors off, and then Ulysses returned, and she said: "Precious husband, I have been faithful in my love and thou art returned." And when the soul gets to the point where it says: "I am honest, I will stay in my devotions, I will leave and turn off every other suitor—the world, the flesh, and the devil—I will turn them all off and keep them at bay; I will look for the coming of my Lord, and I will keep them off until He does come"—oh, that is longing—and longing for Christ!

And then this being in Christ Jesus presupposes another thing. It presupposes fleeing to Christ. Oh, brother, you better not let the grass grow up in the pathway between you and the cross—between you and Christ. Oh, safe is that soul that always knows its way to Christ, and always keeps the path beaten out between it and Christ. Fleeing to Christ—this idea we get from the criminal law. Under the old regime, when a man committed an offense, the one question with him was, "Can I make the city of refuge?" and he dropped all things and he left all things and pressed with all his might to the city of refuge, and as soon as his hands reached the gatepost and he got inside the city, there was no power to arrest him or punish him. And so when the soul has sinned against Christ, then the only question that comes up at all is: "Can I make the city of refuge?" The great St. Paul said: "If any man sin we have an advocate with the Father—even Jesus Christ, the righteous."

Fleeing to Christ! Look here, if I wanted to make the powers of Satan tremble; if I wanted to put to flight all the armies of hell, I would not order ten legions of angels from the skies and all the artillery of heaven turned loose on him.

Do you know what I'd do? I would just fall down on my knees and pray, for

> Satan trembles when he sees
> The weakest saint upon his knees.

And no man was ever conquered on his knees in prayer to God. I have been at the point where I could not do anything but pray; and, blessed be God, that's all I needed to do—just kneel down and pray. On my knees I have worked out problems and settled difficulties that I never could have settled on my feet. Fleeing to Christ! And that's what prayer is. He knows where you break down. He knows which wheel is broken and how many wheels are broken down. He knows whether it is the axle or whether it is the wheel. He knows whether it is the tongue of your wagon or whether it is simply a spoke of one of your wheels. Blessed be God! When I run to Him He can put His finger on the affected part, and He is a balm in Gilead to heal all my diseases and to rearrange all my breakages. Run to Christ! I can get along without anything better than prayer. Prayer is the communion of the soul with God. I can get along without everything but prayer. I am willing that you take almost everything in the world away from me but prayer. Leave me the privilege of rushing to God with prayer, and I shall make my way to heaven.

And, again, being in Christ Jesus presupposes submission to Christ. Now, it is one thing to long for Him, another thing to run to Him in time of danger, and quite another thing to speak to Him when you get there. There are some mysterious things about the Bible. You say, "Submit to Christ! What do you mean?" I mean this: Whatever He says do, you do it. Whatever He says thou oughtest not to do, you let it alone. That is what I mean.

One of the soldiers in the last war told me a story which has an interesting application here. He said: "Jones, I fought in one hundred battles. I have faced the musket and the cannon as they flashed in my face, but the hardest thing I had to do during the war was to obey the order to lie down. Every man fell on his face, and the shell and shot just whizzed and buzzed over our forms as we lay sheltered there. The hardest thing I had to do during the whole war was to lie still under fire, but if I had got up I would have been riddled with bullets in a minute." Now, when Almighty God lets loose His grape and cannister you had better lie low, you had. And every bullet hole you have in your body to-day, you have because you would not be still. That is it.

You say, "Jones, why don't you preach against stealing, lying, and drunkenness?" It is because that ain't hurting the church. Nobody has any respect for you old red-nosed devils in the church. Nobody has any respect for you if you are a liar. Nobody bothers with you if you steal. Nobody cares anything about you. I will tell you it ain't lying, stealing and drunkenness that is cursing the church and paralyzing her power and ruining the Church of God. It is these worldly amusements that are sweeping over our homes and churches, and paralyzing us and making us to-day little better than a graveyard. That is it.

I never saw a spiritual man in my life who would stand up and ask me, "Do you think there is any harm in the dance?" Why don't you ask me if I think there is any harm in a prayer meeting, or if I think there is any harm in family prayer? You know there ain't. And whenever you hear a fellow asking if there is any harm in the dance you can reply, "You lying old rascal, you know there is."

Submission! Oh, the wisest spirit ever manifested by mortal man is that spirit that first said, "I will be loyal to Him, and then lie still under fire. I will be loyal. Though He slay me, I will hope while I live."

And I will say this much. My Christianity has done this much for me. Hear me now, every one of you. I can say it, I think, as truthfully as I ever said anything. I have danced many a night. I have played cards a little. I never got much interested in them, for I think card-playing is the game of starvelings, mental and spiritual. If I had children that would not read a book, and would not be interested in anything that ought to be interesting to intelligent beings,

I would teach them all to play cards. If I had a daughter that was such a simpleton that she had only just sense enough to behave herself, I would send her to a hook-nosed French dancing-master, and I would tell him to make her graceful, and say: "Her head's a failure, and I want you to make it up on the feet." The law of compensation, of checks and balances, ought to work here, ought it not? I would say to the hook-nosed Frenchman, "Bring her feet up right. She is a failure in her head." I would teach her to dance gracefully, and marry her off to some ballroom dude and buy them a place away off in the country and tell them never to come to see me. When I got anxious to see them I would take her mother and go and see them.

A Methodist mother, taking her innocent children, and placing them in the care and under the training of an old hook-nosed Frenchman—the mean old devil—teaching people his manners! I have a contempt for that sort of people, and maybe the rascal has not been out of jail three months before coming here and starting his dancing school. Oh, if I have a contempt for a being in this universe that I cannot reach down to, it is a dancing master. His only business is to go about the community despoiling the spiritual interest of children and making them fall in love with giddy worldliness and foolishness that will damn them in the end. I have made many of them get in places where I have preached. I have gone into towns of ten thousand and fifteen thousand where such a fellow has a grand dancing school, and I would not want more than forty-eight hours to bring him up. I would shell the woods for him a time or two and then you'd see him start hitting the ground about a mile a minute.

Submission! Submission! It means if I swear loyalty to

103

the right I will submit to it. No matter what it costs me, no matter what criticisms are brought to bear on me, I will do right, I will do right. Let people say he is a dolt; let people say he is simple, and that he has no better sense than to be religious. God bless you, there are a good many people in this world who have got just enough sense to be religious, and you will find on the day of judgment that they are the only sensible people in town—those fellows that had just sense enough to be religious. Submission! Submission! I will do right because it is right, and I will not do wrong if I know it. That is what every Christian ought to say. Now, if worldlings and non-members of the church want to do otherwise we say it is in a line with their professions, but we do not want church members to follow in that line.

Submission! The idea is this: "Speak, Lord, thy servant heareth; thou art true and just. Oh, God, speak out and I will hear it, and when I hear I will obey." That is what I mean by submission. I think every Christian man in the world ought to give himself up as fully to God as one of those grand Roger engines gives itself up to the engineer. I have stood on those engines, and as I talked with the engineer I have seen him stand with his hand on the throttle and his eye on the track. Presently he would pull his watch out and look at it quietly. Then I would see him pull the throttle a little wider open, as much as to say, "Give me six or eight more miles an hour—we are getting a little behind." And I have seen him as he approached a station, shut the throttle off, drop the lever forward and stop the engine right where he wanted to stop it. I think every Christian man should turn his soul over to God, just as the engine turns its throttle over to the engineer, and say: "Oh, Lord, if I get a little behind, open my soul and

I will move faster, or if I am going too fast, all you have to do is to shut me off a little and I will slacken my speed."

Submission, being in Christ Jesus, presupposes, lastly, affinities that control my nature in such a way that I am alike in every sense. I have gone into a room where there were a husband and wife who had been living together for fifty years and more. They had just had their golden wedding. I sat down and looked at them a few minutes, and I said, "Well, well, that man and his wife look as much like brother and sister as any two people I have seen in my life. Did you ever see brother and sister more alike than that man and his wife?" Then I commenced to talk to them and said: "Well, well, the very intonations of their voices are just alike." Then directly the old lady said so and so, and the old man said: "I was just going to ask that myself," and I thought to myself: "Not only do they look alike, not only are the intonations of their voices alike, but they think alike." Brother and sister, may our affinities lead us to where we not only look like good men, but where the very intonations of our voices are molded by the spirit of the Master. And not only that, but when you speak out and say, "Blessed are the pure in heart, for they shall see God," it will be said, "He talks like Christ talked. He looks like a good man, and I could have told he was a good man anywhere." Oh, brethren, do not lose any time in hungering for the right, in looking for the right, and in submitting to the right, until you get right from head to foot and you become a big bundle of rightness.

And if any man wants to be made whole, if you feel your weakness, go to Him of whom I have been talking. He is approachable, He is available to every one of you, and the highway that leads to Him is a wide one, open to every soul here. I just want to tell you this in conclusion. Fourteen years ago last August there was an occurrence in my life that reminded me very much of an event that occurred when Christ was on earth. You recollect that once He got on board a little ship with His disciples and started across the Lake of Gennesaret. That little lake was hemmed in with mountains that towered hundreds of feet around it, and it seemed to be secure from the winds. At times, however, furious storms came, and it seemed as if the four winds of heaven were striving to see which should have charge of that little lake. The winds came rushing and bearing down on the lake that time, and the waves began to roll and the water was lashed into foam. The little vessel rocked and pitched and creaked under the pressure of the waves, and the disciples, affrighted, ran and waked the Master and said: "Master, we are engulfed, we are destroyed forever." Jesus looked at the terrific storm. How the vessel shook and pitched, and how the disciples trembled with fear. The Master awoke and wiped the spray from His forehead, and walked to the prow of the little ship. He reached down and pulled the angry wave on His knee and dandled it to sleep like a mother would an infant child. And the disciples said: "Oh, what a calm!"

One day, fourteen years ago, with my soul pitched and tossed and driven by the storms of temptation, I rushed right into His presence. He took me up and pulled me to His great loving heart, and He said: "My peace I give unto thee," and I went away, saying: "Now blessed be God; not a wave of trouble rolls across my peaceful breast." Oh, brother, here is a calm. The soul that was in the midst of storms all its life is enjoying that blessed calm to-day. Oh, Christ, give us the words that will bring a calm to every soul. Now we are going to dismiss you with the benediction, but before we dismiss you we make this proposition: I want every Christian man in this house—I do not care of what church you are a member, and if you have no church, you can accept the proposition—to say: "God helping me, I intend to be a more circumspect Christian, and I am going to do better"; or you can say: "I am going to do my best." I like that sort of fellow. Heaven is just on the other side of a fellow that is doing his best. I want every professor of religion in this house, I do not care whether he is a preacher or a member of the church, or whether in the church or not, if you want to glorify God with a pure, thankful, loyal love, I want every one of you to stand up with me—and do not stand up unless you mean it—and breathe a prayer to God to keep you faithful unto death. (All in the church rose.) Well, thank God, what a host. Now, if there is a nonprofessor who hears the prayers of these people, and you will stand up, we will pray for you the best we can. Thank God, nearly everybody stands up. I think you mean it; you look as if you mean it. Now, blessed Lord God, baptize us in that resolution; fasten it on us, and may we be faithful from this hour until God shall say: "It is enough, come up higher."

What the alphabet is to a man of learning, repent-ance is to a man going to heaven.

S. J.

.

6. REPENTANCE NOT
A MYSTERY

We select as our text on this occasion the 9th verse of the first chapter of John's First Epistle:

> If we confess our sins, he is faithful and just to forgive us our sins, and to cleanse us from all unrighteousness.

This is an epitome of the Gospel. It is wonderful how the apostle could put the whole Gospel into three lines like this. I mean the whole of the Gospel on the human side of the Gospel, and I dare say at this point that the only side of the Gospel that you and I have to do with at all is the human side. In the great work of redemption I have but one question to ask: "Lord, what wilt thou have me to do?" I'll never stop to ask God what He is going to do and how He is going to do it and when He is going to do it; but the question that engages my mind is, "Lord, what wilt thou have *me* to do?" I never preach on the divine side of the Gospel. The water is deep out there, and little boats ought to stay near the shore. I'd want to be a first-class swimmer if I should go out in the depths of divine mysteries and inquire of God what are the divine plans and the divine modes and the divine "when" and the divine "how." These are questions that never bother me at all. I simply want to know what God wants *me* to do, and if He'll tell me I'll do that and trust Him for the rest.

And now St. John gives us clearly and pointedly our side of the gospel in these words: "If we confess our sins, he is faithful and just to forgive us our sins, and to cleanse us from all unrighteousness."

Suppose we read the text this way—and we do no violence to the sense of the text: "If we repent of our sins, he is faithful and just to forgive us our sins, and to cleanse us from all unrighteousness."

In every moral spiritual sense, repentance to a man in this world, on his way to God, is just what the alphabet is to the man of letters and to the scholar. We see that little boy four years old standing at his mother's knee. She is teaching him the alphabet, just as my mother taught me the alphabet. And when I learned the alphabet so that I could begin at "A" and go to "Z," and commence with "Z" and go back to "A," then mother would put her finger at the middle of the alphabet and start me up and down, and I learned the alphabet perfectly and I knew my A B C well. Then my mother turned the leaf and said: "Now, son, you may spell some." And I thought in my little heart: "Well, I'll leave my A B C the first week." So I turned over to the next page and commenced to spell, but I saw before I spelt a word that I could not spell without my A B C, and the first word was "a—b, ab," and "i—ib, ib," and I saw that I couldn't spell without my letters, and I spelled on, and she taught me on till I got over to "baker," and "that's a good way," I thought, but I found I couldn't spell "baker," without the "b" and the "a" and the "k" and the "e" and the "r." And I went on until I got way over to "publication," without the "p" and the "u" and the "b," and so on. Well, after I had started to school and got through the spelling book, my teacher said: "Now, tell your mother to get you a first reader." "Well," I thought "good-by A B C, I am done with you now," but when I opened my first reader, the first page of my first reader was covered with the alphabet, and I couldn't read a line without the alphabet.

And so I went through the first, second, and third readers, and then my teacher said, "Now, you must get you an arithmetic." "Well," I thought, "I'm in arithmetic. That's the science of numbers, and I won't have any alphabet in that. It's 'good-by, alphabet,' now." And I opened my arithmetic and found they couldn't state a mathematical proposition or question without the alphabet, and I went on and on, and by and by they said, "Now, we'll put you into geography."

"Well," said I, "that geography might give me some idea of this earth's surface, and I won't have any alphabet in that," but I found my geography, every page of it, was covered with the alphabet. And by and by I went into rhetoric, and into philosophy, and on and on, and after a while they said, "We'll put you in Latin." "Well," I thought, "in Latin I'll never be troubled with the alphabet," but I found I needed the alphabet when I took up my Latin grammar; and so I progressed in learning, and when I went into Greek they called the letters by different names, but I found out at last that we needed the alphabet in the Greek. And on and on as I go, I need the alphabet, and when the student shall end his college course and his diploma is given him, why, his very diploma is written in the alphabet; and so the higher he climbs in literature and the higher heights he reaches, the more he appreciates the fact that every step of his upward way is made through and by the alphabet.

Well, now, just exactly what the alphabet is to the man of letters, so is repentance to the man on his way to God. The first religious thing a man ever did in this world was to repent, and as far as I am concerned, I have been repenting every day since I started; and the last thing I want to do is to kneel down in hearty repentance before God and go to heaven a sinner saved by grace.

Repentance! Well, we'll take the term of the text: "If we confess our sins, he is faithful and just to forgive us our sins, and to cleanse us from all unrighteousness."

Now, here is a plain, pointed declaration from the lips of God: "If we confess our sins."

I like the term "confess." It is a very potent, significant term in the sense in which this text uses it. "Repentance" cannot mean more than "confession" means in this text. We might understand "repentance" better. We are more familiar with the discussion of that word "repentance," and yet, after all the definitions of "repentance" I have seen in the book, a good old woman gave me the best definition of repentance I ever heard.

I was out talking with her on religion and she said to me: "Brother, I'll tell you what repentance is."

Said I, "What?"

Said she, "It is being so sorry for your meanness that you ain't going to do it any more."

"Well," said I, "you've got it down right for certain."

There's no such definition in the books as that. And she said: "I'll tell you what religion is."

Said I, "What?"

She said: "If God will forgive me for my meanness I won't want to do it any more."

"Well," said I, "now you have got the whole question in a nutshell."

Repentance is this: "I am so sorry for my meanness that I won't do it any more," and religion is, "I am so glad that God is so good to forgive me that I won't want to do it any more."

Confession! I have noticed this fact in my experience, that a man's reformation will always go down as deep and out as broad as his confession is. An honest confession, it is said, is good for the soul, and a man is never willing to confess until he is willing to quit.

Now, let me illustrate what I mean: You may take any drunkard; let him confess his sins to God and man, let him quit and let him join the church and serve God, and at every experience meeting you have that fellow will jump up and say, "Brethren, glory to God! I was saved from a drunkard's grave!" He has quit. There's another fellow, he hasn't quit—you can tell it by his nose, and you say: "Friend, do you drink?"

"No, sir! I don't know one sort from another. I never drank a drop in my life."

What's the matter with him? He hasn't quit, you see. And no man is ready to confess until he is ready to quit.

You take a gambler, a notorious gambler, and let him be converted to God and join the church, and all at once he gets up and says: "Brethren, I have been the worst gambler. I have gambled every day. I have gambled all night many a time. I have led a miserable gambler's life." Well, you take one of the blacklegs of the city now and get him up here and say: "Do you gamble?"

"No, sir! I don't know one card from another. Never played a game in my life."

What's the matter with him? He hasn't quit, don't you see?

And there is one peculiarity about sin. It not only makes

113

a fool of a man, but it will make him a fraud. About nine-tenths or eleven-tenths of the lying done in this world is to get out of something we have done that is wrong. Isn't that true? How many men in this house who drink whisky can stand up and say, "I never told my wife a lie about it in my life"? How many drinking men can stand up and say, "I am a regular steady drinker, but I never told my wife a falsehood about it in my life"? There isn't one drunkard in fifty that will confess to how much he does drink. There isn't one gambler in fifty who will ever confess to God or man the gambler's life that he leads. And the best proof in the world that a man has reformed is the fact of his confessing his guilt before God and man.

Or, to illustrate further, I recollect that once, while I was pastor, I had two members up in the church for drunkenness. One fellow got up and said: "Brethren, I went to town the other day, and I didn't eat any dinner and I took one little drink. It flew to my head and made me sort of tight, and I hope you'll all forgive me." Well, the church forgave him, but as he went out of the door I said to the brethren: "That fellow will get drunk again the first time he goes to town!"

They said: "How do you know?"

"Well," said I, "he told two or three lies in his short confession. Did you notice that? He said he just took one little drink, and that wouldn't make anybody but a fool drunk, in the first place; and, in the second place, he said it made him 'sort of tight,' and, from all I can hear, he is the loosest fellow that has been floating round lately. He told two pointblank lies in one little confession, and he'll get drunk again the first time he goes to town again."

And, sure enough, he did.

The other one got up and said: "Brethren, if I may call

114

you such, I went to town and I made a brute of myself. I disgraced myself and the Christ that I profess." And, said he, "If you all can bear with me and forgive me, I want you to pray for me and help me. I have been begging God to forgive me, and if you can bear with such a wretch as I, I hope you will, and pardon me this time."

I said to them, after he went out: "I'll go his security. I'll go on his bond almost with my immortality, if such a thing is necessary. He has grit."

"How do you know?" they said.

"Why," said I, "he confessed to the bottom, and when a man gets down to the bottom in his confession he is reformed to the bottom."

Confession! Repentance! It means nothing more than this: "I have quit! I have done!" Repentance don't mean blubbering and crying. Here's a poor fellow now who's been getting drunk every day for a month. He comes home at nights blubbering and tells his wife: "Sho sorry (hic) I got drunk; but—" and it's boo, boo, and cry and cry. "I'm so sorry I got drunk to-day. Wifey, I h-ope you'll for-give me."

And the next day he goes right down town and gets drunk again, and comes home drunk, and he'll blubber and he'll cry. Well, you see, blubbering ain't the thing at all, and his wife gets disgusted with him, and tells him: "You needn't come round me with your blubbering. I despise it, I despise it. It doesn't amount to anything in the world."

But he comes home sober one evening, and he says, with his eyes light and all his senses in full play: "Wife, I have quit and done now. I'll never drink another drop while God lets me live."

Well, he don't blubber about it a bit. That's just what

115

his wife wanted—just waiting for him to quit, that was all. And a man needn't think because he comes to Christ snubbing around the altar, "I'm the best penitent they have had," and then go to snubbing and crying. But it's, "I have quit, quit." That's it. "I have done with it." Repentance is reformation, and nothing is repentance except reformation.

Suppose you had a boy who was going into wickedness and prodigality and intemperance, and going on and on in that, what would you care for your boy coming to you every day or two and shedding tears and saying: "I am so sorry, father, I have done this way"? You would just straighten him up and look at him and say: "Son, you needn't come blubbering around me; you just quit, and when you are quit there's no use blubbering, and you needn't blubber until you quit."

God is my Father and I am His child. And what does the Lord want me to do in every sense? Brother, let you and I cease to do evil and learn to do well. Let the wicked man cease his way and come to God, and God will pardon him.

How much mystery we have wrapped up with this thing we call religion! The Lord wants every guilty man in the world to quit his wickedness, turn away from his sins, and then come to God, and he shall have eternal life. The devil don't want any better joke on a preacher than to get up in the pulpit and split a hair a whole mile long between evangelical repentance and legal repentance. The devil is always glad when he sees a man giving his whole time to that kind of thing. And there is that preacher, and he is defining repentance now and is giving the world his views of evangelical repentance and legal repentance. I say to the world—and it is the message of my Lord and Master—

"If you want God to take hold of you, you quit! you quit! you quit!"

Well, many a time we members of the church get very sorry, and we get so sorry we can shed some tears for our past life. Now, let me speak a word to you brother, sister. There is a brother who is neglecting his family altar; he has let the family altar fires go out and he is neglecting his duty as a father, as a husband, and now he comes up to the Lord here and says: "Oh, Lord, I have been a great sinner. Forgive me for Christ's sake." And he sheds a great many tears, but he don't take up his family prayer, he don't make any repentance in the world. Brother, you need not get up out of your seat, but sit right there and say: "I am sorry I have neglected the family altar, and, God helping me, I will quit my neglect and follow up my family prayers until God calls me to him."

There is another brother who says: "I have not been to a prayer meeting for a year." Brother, you need not cry about it, but say, "God helping me, I am going to be out here every Wednesday night to the prayer meeting, else I will send my doctor's certificate to my preacher, and show I was sick abed and couldn't come."

We have theories enough; we have all sorts of theories, and plenty of theories to run one hundred worlds. What we want now is something practical—something that means something.

A fellow has done wrong, has swindled a customer, and is feeling awful bad about it; he never felt so bad in his life. Now, brother, it doesn't matter how you feel. Are you willing to take the overplus back home to your brother and say, "Here is what I overcharged you with," or will you keep it? There is something practical about that. I like the sort of feeling a fellow felt when he heard that a neighbor's cow had died, and he said to the other neighbors: "Oh, how sad it is! I am so sorry for it." "How sorry do you feel? Ten dollars' worth to help him get another cow?" I like to see a fellow's sorrow take a turn on him and manifest itself in a practical way, don't you see?

And that's what's the matter with the world to-day. They are looking for a practical test in our Christianity; and they just simply think that religion is confined to the meeting-house and to our connection with the church. Oh, brethren, let us teach this world there is something grander and nobler about religion than simply a few mysterious theories about a person or a substance. That is it.

Repentance! Confession! I am never troubled much about a man when he says to me, "Jones, I have made up my mind to quit everything that God's book condemns. I will never do it again." I get very hopeful of that sort of a fellow; and when he says to me, "Well, I haven't got any feeling," I say to him, "What do you want to talk about feeling for? Who said anything about feeling? The Lord said: 'Let the wicked man forsake his way and the unrighteous man his thoughts.' And here you are, after you know what the Lord wants you to do, you are growling about feeling. Where do you get that idea? Where does that come from?" Brethren, I say to you, if there is nothing in religion but feeling, I haven't got a bit, for if I have any feeling in me to-night I couldn't locate it to save my life.

Feeling! You know the difference between feeling and principle? Yonder is an old sailboat out in the middle of the Atlantic Ocean, and when the wind blows, why, she travels ten miles an hour; but let the wind lull and she will lie there two weeks within one hundred yards of where the wind left her. She don't go anywhere. That is feeling. When the wind blows, off she goes.

What is principle? Yonder is a grand old ocean steamer, and when the wind blows she spreads her sails and works her steam and on she goes, and when the wind lulls the engineer turns his throttle wider open and she goes at the rate of fifteen miles an hour, whether the wind blows or not. And that is the difference between principle and feeling. And if I haven't got any more feeling this side of eternity, I am going to serve God and do right because it is right, and I won't do wrong, because it is wrong. A man that's hunting for feeling!

And we have taught this world a great many strange ideas about religion from the pulpit. There is a sort of a semi-infidel. He is a little fellow. He has never grown much. But he thinks, "Well, from what I heard the preacher say, there ain't any hope for me. I am shut out of the pale; no hope for me, because I don't believe a heap of things in the Bible," and he thinks he is ruined because he don't. I strike a heap of these little infidels that want religion, and I never struck any of the sort except these small ones. He says he wants to be a Christian, but he don't believe that Jonah swallowed the whale, and he don't believe that the three Hebrew children went into the fiery furnace, and he don't believe in these big fish tales, and I just say to him, "You poor, little, simple-headed thing, God never said 'Give me your head,' or 'Give me your feet,' but 'Give me your heart,' and God knows your little, old persimmon head is chock-full of devilment. He never bothers about your head. He doesn't say 'Give me your head,' but He says 'Give me your heart,' and God will comb the kinks out of your head mighty fast if you will just give Him your heart." He is just one of those "end fiddles," as the boys call him, and he just thinks because his little head is chock-full of little things for a great many years, that will make the Lord turn away from him in despair.

Why, brother, when my boy gets wrong notions in his head, that don't make me hate my boy. I just turn to him and say: "My son, if you will submit yourself to my discipline I will promise you a pure life. And I will say this to you: 'Your head will get right when I get your life straight.'" A man don't do like he believes, but he believes like he does. Don't you see?

Here is a man talking about doubts. I never had anything but doubts in my life. And if you want to get doubt out of your heart you go right down and pull it up by the roots, and there is a seed at the bottom of that top root, and the name of that seed is sin.

And I will say to you all that the best cure on earth for infidelity is for a fellow to just go on living the pure precepts of the Bible and his head will become straight. A man cannot start head foremost toward God. He will strike a hard substance and break his old head. You start heart foremost—that's the way. A man goes heart foremost toward God—and that's the way to go. God says: "Give me thine heart—give me thine heart."

Down in one of the towns in a Southern State a man— some of you know the man if I were to call his name—got interested in the meeting and came to me and said: "Mr. Jones, I really in my heart want to be a good man, but I don't believe in the divinity of Christ—I can't to save my life—and I want to be a good man."

Said I, "Do you?"

He said, "Yes."

"Well," said I, "to-night when I open the doors of the church, you come up and join the church."

"What!" said he, "me join the church, Mr. Jones, and I don't believe in the divinity of Christ!"

Said I, "Your trouble is your mouth. If you just shut your mouth I will just get you straight in twenty-four hours."

"Now," said I, "to-night you come up and join the church."

"Why,—"

"Now, just listen to that mouth. It has been your trouble all your life and you'll just talk yourself into hell if you don't shut your mouth. Now, when I open the doors to-night, you come up and say, 'The best I can do is to give my heart to God.'"

"Why, Mr. Jones,—"

"You don't open your mouth. You don't understand. You just shut your mouth and I will get you all straight."

"Well," said he, "I cannot,—"

"Now," said I, "just listen to that. You will talk yourself into the pit."

And next day I met him and he said: "Mr. Jones, I have been thinking very seriously of what you said, but my head is not straight; I cannot believe right."

"Well," said I, "you just shut your mouth and go and do just like a Christian ought to do and you will come out straight."

Well, that night, to my utter astonishment, that fellow came up, trembling, and joined the church, and he said to me the next day: "Now, sir, Mr. Jones, when they ask me whether I believe in God the Father Almighty, maker of heaven and earth, and in Jesus Christ, his only Son, our Lord—when they ask me that, what must I say?"

Said I: "You shut your mouth, and if you won't talk I will get you straight—just shut your mouth for about forty-eight hours."

And he came through as happy a Christian man as I

know in all this land. But it was a hard matter with him. His head was wrong, and he put his tongue in charge of his head and he was talking himself to perdition.

Did you ever see an infidel in your life that could sit still and be quiet when he once got going? That's the way he's going.

Repentance! I will quit! I will quit! I will cease to do evil! I will learn to do good! The best way in the world to get religion is to do, before you get religion, just what you think you will do after you get it.

An incident of that sort happened in Georgia. It is told of one of our best men. He was a married man; he was young, and he came to church one day and his wife was not with him, and when the brother had preached the word, he stood up, for that preacher had said in his sermon, "If a man will do before he gets religion like he thinks he will do after he gets it, he will get it." When he was through preaching, the preacher opened the door of the church and this man walked right up and joined the church. He went home and his wife said: "What sort of a meeting did you have?"

He said, "We had a splendid meeting and I joined the church."

"You joined the church?"

"Yes."

"Have you got religion?"

"No."

"Well, what in the world did you join the church for before you got religion?"

"Well," he said, "the preacher said if I'd do before I got religion like I thought I ought to do after I got religion to come up and join the church, and I joined it."

"Well," she said, "that's a mighty strange way to me."

122

That night before going to bed, he said:

"Wife, get the Bible. I'm going to read a chapter and have family prayer."

"What are you going to do that for and you ain't got religion?"

"Well, the preacher said if I wanted to get religion to do before I got religion as I thought I would do after I got religion, and you know if I was a Christian I'd have family prayers in my house every night."

And before breakfast the next morning he told his wife to get the Bible, that he was going to pray again, and she said: "You are the strangest man I ever saw, to pray in your family when you have not got any religion."

And he went on and on, and the next Wednesday night she went to the prayer meeting with him, and at the prayer meeting the preacher called on him to pray, and he knelt down and prayed the best he could, and after he got out of church his wife took his arm and she said: "Ain't you a nice man to pray in public and got no religion! What in the world did you do that for, husband?"

"Well," he said, "the preacher told me if I would do before I got religion as I thought I ought to do after I got religion, I would get religion, and I know that Christians pray in public."

And he just kept right on, on that line, for three weeks, and the biggest case of religion broke out on him of any man in all that part of the country.

A man cannot live religiously without being religious, and a man cannot be religious without living religiously. It works both ways. It is just as certain that Pine Street leads down to Fourth Street, and just as certain that the way of grace will take a man to God. Just as certain as the L. and N. Railroad leads from St. Louis to Nashville, just so certain is the plain naked test that God imposes on man will take any man to God and heaven.

I wish we could eliminate from religion everything we call mysterious. We ministers get up in the pulpit and we mystify and bamboozle the world with this thing that we call religion. I used to hear the Christian people get up and talk about the birds singing sweeter and the trees looking brighter, and everything like that, after they got religion. I just thought it was something, and how magnificent it was, until I read it in a book one day, and I wondered ever since if that old brother got it out of that book.

If birds sing more sweetly and trees look prettier after a fellow gets religion, I never had religion. Birds always sang sweetly and trees always looked pretty to me. There is not a word in the Bible about birds and trees, but there is a heap in there about quitting meanness and learning to do well.

Repentance! Repentance! I think I never in my experience as a preacher found a soul that was willing to give up sin, give up all sin, and stay at that point with the white flag run up, that God did not go to that soul. I recollect in my own experience I thought I had cried a heap, and I thought I had mourned a heap, and I went along, mourning and crying, and I gave up such sins that I thought I could get on best without, and when I quit crying and mourning and threw my sins down in one bundle I did not go fifteen steps until I was conscious God was my friend and that He was my Saviour. How did they get religion when Christ was on earth? He saw Zaccheus up a sycamore tree. I don't know what he was doing there. But Christ saw him. Zaccheus was a rich fellow, and I expect he had pretty high notions, and Christ said to him, "Come down, Zaccheus, this day salvation has entered your house." And

Zaccheus started down that tree, and got religion some-where between the lowest limb and the ground. At any rate, he had it before he hit the ground. He said: "What I have taken wrongfully from any man I will restore it to him fourfold. He had a good case of religion in him when he hit the ground, there is no doubt of that.

If we repent of our sins, and if you quit doing wrong and determine upon the right, God will meet you. Bishop Marvin said that repentance was "the first conscious move-ment of the soul from sin toward God," and he said that after a man threw down his sins and walked off from them, no matter in what direction he started, he started God-ward, and the farther you walked off from sin, the closer you got to God, and a man can go back, and gather up his sins and start the other way and every way is hellward and downward. It is not so much the direction you are going in, but what sort of a fellow you are and what you have got with you.

Repentance! Repentance! I wish I could get you to see, my friends, that God is the common Father of us all, and that God loves the worst of us as much as He loves the best of us. God only asks us to, "cease to do evil and to learn to do well." If we would confess our sins He is faith-ful and just to forgive us our sins. Well, we need the par-don. We ought to be pardoned, but we need something besides pardon. We need cleansing from all unrighteous-ness. Let me illustrate this.

Yonder is a man in jail. He is sentenced by the court to hang on the third Friday of next month. Now, last night he broke out with confluent smallpox. The impending execution is over him and he knows that the third Friday of next month he is going to be hung, and last night he broke out with confluent smallpox. Now, if the doctor cures him he will be hung. If the Governor pardons him he will die of smallpox. He is in a bad fix, ain't he? Can you imagine any worse?

Here is a sinner. If God would pardon me for all my past offenses and leave me corrupt in heart, I would just go on and die as inevitably from spiritual disease as that poor criminal will die of smallpox. Now, what do I want? Lord God, thou great Governor of the universe, give me pardon for all my past offenses, and then cleanse me from all unrighteousness, that I may lead a better, nobler, and purer life. The man who is simply pardoned and turned loose is just like a swine. You may take and wash the swine from head to foot with Pears' soap, if you please, and it won't be an hour before it is in another mudhole. And you can take that drunkard out there, wipe out all his past offenses, pardon him for every drunk he ever got on, and just watch him stagger to-morrow evening. Now, what did he want? He wanted not only pardoning for his past misdoing, but he wanted God Almighty to cleanse his heart and mind so that he would never go into another barroom or take another drink. Now, hear me; I am talking perfectly dispassionately and am perfectly honest with every man of you.

You take my friend sitting on my right, my friend Small. There he sits, controlled and governed by a passion that was as remorseless as death. It swept through his soul almost with the power of a cyclone. The day after his pardon, the day after he felt, "God has forgiven all my past sins," this thirst for drink came on him with all its power and energy, and he went to his room and dropped on his knees and said, "Oh, my God, I can never take a step out of my house; I can never go out on the streets of this city with such an appetite gnawing within me." He fought there with that appetite for two solid hours, and he said, "God Almighty came down and helped me to struggle with that thirst, and from that moment to this I have never had any desire to take another drink." I believe that just as strongly as I believe that I am here to-night. I have been along there myself.

Now, I want to tell you this old race needs something else besides pardon for the little meannesses it has already committed. This old race needs cleansing, and God has promised that he will not only pardon our past, but that he will cleanse us from all sin. Is there any man here to-night who will say, "God helping me, I will quit; I am done; I know what sin is; I will quit"? If you do that, brother, you have taken the one step that brings you into the latitude where God can get hold of you.

Now, here is a naked promise of God: "If we confess our sins, he is faithful and just to forgive us." And now let us put ourselves honestly and squarely on this one promise. The stockmen of the West, in order to prevent cattle from wading into the pools in their pastures and making the water muddy, have built a rock wall about the pools, and put a platform over the pool, and put a trough on the side of the platform. The trough cannot be seen from the outside, and I expect that if an old ox were to rear up and look over the platform, he would tell the others, "There is not a drop of water in that trough. I can see it, and there is not a drop of water in it." Mr. Tyndall got up there and looked down, and he said, "There is nothing in it." But that old ox, thirsty for water, walks around the wall and onto that platform, and the pressure of his weight on the platform forces the water, sparkling and gurgling, up into the trough, and he drinks and is never dry. Brother, this naked promise of God is right over the pools of the water of life, and these scientific gentlemen have, somehow, seen down into the trough and said: "There is not a drop of water in it." They are right about that; but let the poor sinner walk out on the platform, and his weight will force the water of life into the trough, and he will drink and rejoice in the fact that religion is true.

My little Bob, when he was five years old, had more religious sense than I had when I was twenty-four. I went home one day, and when I went into the house, I said, "Wife, where are the children?" She said, "Brother George Smith is preaching to the children, and our little fellow was much interested and had to go." And we sat and talked awhile, and directly little Bob came running in. I took him on my lap, and his mother talked to him. She said: "Robert, what sort of a meeting did you have?"

"We had a good meeting."

"What did you do?"

"Mr. Smith preached a good sermon and asked us to go to the altar."

"Did you go, Bob?"

"Yes, ma'am."

"What did you go for?"

"I wanted to have my sins forgiven."

"Did you get them forgiven?"

"Yes ma'am."

"How do you know?"

"Mr. Smith said if we would come up and ask the Lord to do it He would do it."

"Bob, are you going to sin any more?" asked his mother.

"Yes'm, I expect I will."

"What will you do then?"

"I will wait until Mr. Smith comes around again and go up again."

And the little fellow had the whole thing as clearly in his mind as ever any man had.

"I went up to confess my sins."

"Were you forgiven?"

"Yes."

"How do you know?"

"Because God says if a man will confess He will forgive him."

And that is where God brought us when He said: "Except ye be as little children ye can in no wise enter the kingdom of heaven." And John said: "If we confess our sins, he is faithful and just to forgive us our sins and to cleanse us from all unrighteousness."

I wish this world could see that all a man need do is to repent of his sins and call on God, and he is a pardoned man right then and there.

When I was pastor of a circuit in Georgia a few years ago, I had some fifth Sunday appointment. I preached there the fifth Saturday and Sunday. And the fifth Sunday of March I went over there and preached two days. On the Saturday I went home with a gentleman named Gaither, not a member of the church. He was a well-to-do man, and a graduate of Emory College. I talked with him and said: "Mr. Gaither, you are not a member of the church?"

"No, sir," he said.

"Well," said I, "I want you to join the church to-morrow."

"Why," he said, "Mr. Jones, I cannot join the church. I curse sometimes, and I drink a little."

"That is the reason I want you to join."

"Jones, you don't mean to say that you want a man that will curse and drink to join the church?"

"No, but you are a man of honor and integrity, and if you were to promise God you would quit that sort of thing you would quit it."

But he had made up his mind that he would not join the church until he got religion. Many a fellow has said that he would not know what religion was if he met it in the road. He would ask the first fellow he met afterward what was that? Oh, me, if a man did not have more common sense than he has religious sense he would die in an asylum. Good sense on everything else in the world, but when it comes to religion the biggest lawyer and the blackest and most ignorant Negro stand on the same platform.

Presently his wife came out and I said, "I have been trying to get your husband to join the church, and I want you to join."

"I can never commit the sin of joining the church until I get religion," she said.

I had a long conversation with them on the subject, and I thought I had struck about two of the hardest cases I had ever encountered. I went and preached the next day at 11 o'clock, and on the conclusion of the sermon that man and his wife and eight or ten others walked right up and joined the church. That was the fifth Sunday in March. On the fifth Sunday in July I was back there, preaching three days. On Saturday night wife was with me, and she and the wife of Mr. Gaither went round in the carriage and he and I walked through the fields. We were walking along, talking, and the moon was shining brightly, and I said: "Brother Gaither, old Watt is doing his whole duty" —that was Gaither's brother-in-law, who had also joined the church.

"Yes," was the reply.

"He can't be religious unless he is doing his whole duty," I said.

"Can any man?" he asked.

"Old Watt cannot appear to be religious unless he does his whole duty," I said. Old Watt was a drinking, gambling, bad fellow when he came into the church, but he came all over and taught Sunday school, worked as class leader, and became Sunday-school superintendent, doing his whole duty and loving religion.

Mr. Gaither said: "Yes. Now, what is there in appearances? I have been in the church three months and I have no more religion than that horse pulling our wives to church. I have not cursed any nor drank any since I joined the church; but I am tired of being a member of the church without religion. If you want me to pray to-night I will do my best. If you want me to teach Sunday school I'll do it. I am going to pray night and morning until I get religion. I am going to do it. I want to do my whole duty until I get religion," and suddenly shouting, he said: "Glory be to God, I have got it right here."

That is the secret of the whole thing, brother. Oh that I could just get men to see how merciful God is to the man that wants to do the clean thing.

Now, my brother, my friend, God loves you, and all God asks of any man is that you

Cease to do evil and learn to do well.

And follow in the footsteps of Him who loved you and gave His life for you and died for you. That's it. And there is no mystery about it. When an army official advertises the conditions on which he will receive a regular soldier into the army there is no more mystery about those conditions than when God advertises to the world how He will receive men and women into His Kingdom on earth and into His kingdom in heaven. And turn your minds and thoughts away from the mysteries connected with re-ligion, and just take hold of the plain, practical facts of Christianity and say: "I know right's right and I will do it; and I know wrong is wrong, and I will quit it." Turn your life to God, and He will have mercy on you and pardon you. Will you do it? God help every man not in sympathy with God to-night to say: "Whatever others may do, as for me I am going from this day to trust to my Maker to guide me in the way of everlasting life and peace."

Just as the makers of a piano can put it in tune, God can set the Ten Commandments to music in a man's soul, and all will blend in perfect beauty and harmony.

S. J.

7. GOD'S CALLS AND LOVE

WE INVITE YOUR ATTENTION TO THREE VERSES TO BE found in the first chapter of the Book of Proverbs:

Because I have called and ye refused; I have stretched out my hand, and no man regarded.

But ye have set at naught all my counsel, and would none of my reproof.

I also will laugh at your calamity; I will mock when your fear cometh.

The more I read this precious book I hold in my hand, the more I am persuaded of this one fact, that God is doing all that infinite wisdom and infinite love could do to call back a wandering world to Himself. There is not a page of this blessed book on which I do not find expressions and declarations that convince me in my own mind that God loves me and is interested in me, that God wishes me well, and that He is ever ready to manifest Himself as a gracious benefactor. And when I read this text and look at the pronouns of this text, "Because I have called—" I know this is God speaking, and when God speaks all mankind ought to rise to their feet and listen to what He has to say, "Because I have called and ye—" you and you and you "—and ye refused; I have stretched out my hand, and no man regarded; but have set at naught all my counsel and would none of my reproof. I also will laugh at your calamity; I will mock when your fear cometh."

I said a moment ago that I was more and more persuaded every day that God loves men, that God wishes us well, that He is continually calling us from something and continually calling us to something. Every time God calls a soul from hell He calls that soul to heaven, and when God calls us to heaven He calls us from hell; and when He calls me away from, He calls me up to; and when He calls me up to His bosom He calls me from all that would offend Him or damage me as an immortal man. And now we will discuss the text in a plain, pointed way, and will you give us your prayers and your attention?

Because I have called—Oh, the numberless ways in which God has been calling this world to repentance, calling us to a better life, to nobler things, to higher heights, to greater usefulness, to greater blessedness. And there never has been a call of God to man that did not draw us and bid us come to something better, and something happier, and something wiser, and something grander. There never has been a call of God that did not call us upward. Who is it that does not want to be acquainted with a better state of things? Who is it would not like to see his children on a better and higher plane of right living? Who is it that would not like to see this whole world lifted up into the perennial sunshine and blessing?

Every call of this God-blessed book is a call to us away from something that is wrong toward something that is better. As I hear God and heed Him and obey His commands, I am always leaving that which is bad and going up to that which is better. Do you want to be a better man?

136

God wants you to be. Do you want to be a better woman? God wants you to be. Do you want to be a better father and citizen? God wants you to be. And this old book does not mean anything, from Genesis to Revelation, except that its truths shall make you happier, freer, wiser, purer; and every call in this book is to you and me to come up on a plane like this to something better.

Because I have called—One of the divine agencies and one of the most omnipotent in calling men from sin to righteousness is the divine Spirit. "I have called you by my Spirit." And in His gracious love God sent His Son to die for us. The Son came and took upon Himself to redeem all the race. He suffered, bled and died, and was buried, and He rose again from the dead and said: "It is expedient for you that I go away, for when I go away, the Comforter will come."

And I have thought many times that if God had left this world without the presence and power of His Spirit in the sacrifice of His Son, oh, what an unmeaning sacrifice that would have been! You see that cross yonder, with its bleeding victim, the Saviour of the world, dying upon it, and all mankind gazing upon it. It was the dim outline of something. The world did not understand it. Just as with the hills of North Georgia. Some mornings I have walked out on the front porch of a country residence before daylight and I would look out on the beautiful scenery in the darkness of the night, and I could not see anything but the dim outline of mountains and valleys. It was an indistinct picture that did not mean anything. And I would go back to my room and after a while walk out on the porch again. Then the sun had risen up over the eastern hills and bathed the mountains and valleys in a sea of glorious light.

137

And then I would look over these mountains and valleys and see beauties and glories my mind had not conceived before when I looked at them in the dark.

Then, this old world looked on and did not understand it. It was too dim. But when the Holy Spirit, aglow with the light of God's countenance, arose on the scene and bathed the cross in a sea of light, then we could see

> One hanging on the tree,
>   In agonies of blood,
> Would fix His languid eyes on me,
>   As near His cross I stood.

Then I might say:

> Sure, never to my latest breath,
>   Can I forget that look;
> He seemed to charge me with His death,
>   Though not a word He spoke.

And then:

> My conscience would feel and own the guilt
>   And plunge me in despair;

By that precious light I could see that

> My sins His blood had spilled
>   And helped to nail Him there.
> A second look—

Under this divine light—

> He gave, which said,
>   "I freely all forgive.
> My blood is shed to ransom thee,
>   I die that you may live."

And, oh, the cross itself would never have been anything but a dim outline of God's goodness to us unless the divine

Spirit had bathed it in a sea of light, so that I could see that on that cross was my Redeemer and precious Saviour. Oh, Holy Spirit, arise on the scene to-night and let us see that cross, and see our Saviour, and see that "he is the propitiation for our sins, and not for ours only, but also for the sins of the whole world."

He calls us by His Spirit. His Spirit lights up Calvary and lets us see the bleeding victim. And then the divine Spirit calls us to look on that scene. It calls us to view our Saviour on the cross. It tells us that He is our Saviour and Redeemer. He calls us by His Spirit. And that divine Spirit is going into the World "to reprove men of sin and remind them of righteousness, of judgment to come."

And, brethren, no wonder it is written in that book, "Grieve not the Holy Spirit of God, whereby ye are sealed unto the day of redemption."

I can afford to do anything but treat lightly the wooings and movings of the divine Spirit of Christ.

Oh, brethren, mark the expression! Whatever else you and I do, when by His Spirit God Himself touches our heart, let us yield to that touch and obey that voice! And that divine Spirit is in this city, in this congregation, in your heart. He calls you to a better life. Will you heed that call? Will you obey that call? Whenever the divine Spirit knocks at the door of your heart like He is knocking at some of your hearts to-night, He simply knocks that you may open unto Him, and it brings life and salvation in His train where'er He goes.

He calls us by His Spirit to a better life. I know God is in earnest, because all the manifestations of His grace shows that He has not left a stone unturned to make me a better man. He not only calls me by His Spirit, but by

His word. Do you know how many calls there are in this book to men, that they may live better and serve God and their generation by the will of God?

Have you any idea how many calls there are in this book to you, my brother, and to you, my sister? Oh, this book! with each page, and sometimes with each verse, calling us to nobler and better things! And this book has been on the table at your home, and on the shelf at your home, and in your library at your house, this book, with its millions of copies scattered over the earth, and almost a million calls in each book! Oh, surely no man can sink down to hell at last and say, "I would have gone to nobler heights and to a better life than I did if I had had just one call of mercy and goodness from God to me." This blessed book, how full of calls! Oh, there is many a man who not only despises the God of this book, but despises this book. I love this book. I am glad this book was the precious gift of mother to her children. I am glad my mother clasped this book to her heart and said a thousand times:

> Holy Bible! book divine!
> Precious treasure, thou art mine.

I am so glad my father's highest ambition was to live according to the precepts of this book. I am glad that the noblest and best friends I have in this world have charged me many times to read the word of God, and obey its precepts. I am so glad of the ten millions of Bibles scattered over this sin-cursed earth that go like blessings into every home. And, friends, when we take this blessed book we see the numberless calls God makes to each man. And in each call He says, "Come higher; live better; prepare to meet your God." Then, I say, if we should die impenitent, we are dumb and speechless in the end.

This blessed book, so full of calls! "Come thou," says this book, "come with us and we will do thee good."

But I know God is in earnest. He not only gave His Son and His divine Spirit, but He calls us to a better life, and not only gave His last message to us and His divine counsel to us, but calls us by His ministry. Just think of the numberless voices that are raised every day and every hour on this earth.

The ministry, the consecrated ministry of God! I know frequently we think the preachers are not doing much. We think frequently that "our preacher is a very inefficient man," but I can say this to the honor of our pulpits in America: There is not a soul in this house that ever heard a sermon by anybody—I care not if it was by an old African preacher, I care not what language he spoke—I say to you, you never heard a sermon in your life that did not have truth enough in it to save your soul! We can criticize preachers—oh, me! it takes less sense to criticize than it does to do anything else in the world, and there is many a preacher whose congregation will pack him in an icehouse and then abuse him because he does not perspire. And let me tell you that we would have more faithful preachers and more persistent and earnest work in the pulpit if they got a little sympathy from the world around them.

Sympathy! Say what you please about preachers, I have noticed this much, that, whatever infidelity has done, or whatever infidelity has proposed to do, I have never heard of a project like this would be—an infidel city without a preacher or a church or a Bible. Have you ever heard of any such project as that? The meanest, darkest, blackest old infidel in the world never intends to live among infidels, anywhere in this world, and he is going to be ruined forever, because he is going to be shut up with them in hell forever, and that will be the meanest and most bitter pill he has to swallow down there! The meanest and lowest-down old infidel in this town—if you were going to establish a town of infidels and shut out all preachers and Bibles, and pass a law that no church shall be erected there —there is no low-down infidel in this town that would move his family there or establish himself there if he was an old bachelor. That's the truth.

I declare to you that I have thought many a time if I should be lost, and if I must be lost, I'd rather go from some lonely island of the sea, where no preacher's voice was ever lifted, and where no Bible ever came, and where no influence was ever brought to bear upon me. If I must be lost at last, let me go from some lonely island of the sea, where no voice of the pulpit and no pleading of the church was ever heard. But the man or woman that sinks down to death and hell from under the voice of the pulpit, you perish awfully and you perish justly. "I have called you by my ministry."

Brethren, there has been one sermon to each soul in this city. There have not been less than 400,000 sermons preached in this city since the day it was incorporated. And now, brethren, we are assured of this fact, that for every soul there has been an honest, earnest sermon preached. And, oh, brethren, when I think how Peter ran down that day from that upper chamber and preached one short sermon—and I say it reverently, and I speak it honestly and reverently—you never heard a sermon in your life, I dare assert, that was not as good a sermon in a literal sense as was Peter's sermon on the day of Pentecost. And yet under that short, earnest talk three thousand souls were brought to God. And, with the wagonloads of sermons that have been wasted upon us today, thousands and hundreds of thousands of our people are in the gall of bitterness and in the bonds of iniquity.

I have called you by my ministry. I have sent you my preacher. I have sent preacher after preacher to knock at the door of your conscience and arouse you and awaken you from your lethargy. Thank God for every consecrated preacher that walks the face of the earth! And we will never know how to esteem preachers in this life. The people of this world don't recognize how God Himself has thrown the preacher in the pathway of every man to check him and stop him and turn him around to bring him to God.

And He not only has called us by His ministry. If He had stopped at that, it seems to me that every man who perished would perish without excuse, but He has called us by His providences.

Oh, how the providences of God arouse us and stir us up at times.

In our town, an old associate of mine, an old schoolmate —a kind-hearted, clever boy—and I walked down to his house one day. I heard his child was sick. I walked down to his house and I was invited into the family room. His wife was an old friend of mine—we were boy and girl together. When I went in, she sat in the family room, with a sweet, sick child in her arms, and I looked at that child and I looked at her. I said: "Virginia, God is going to take this little fellow from you, too; he certainly cannot live." And I saw the tears leap to her eyes and spatter down into the face of the sweet child.

Said I: "Virginia, has it ever appeared to you, have you ever thought, that God is doing His best to save your poor husband"—her husband had drunk and drunk and drunk, and he had suffered with delirium tremens but a

143

short time before. "Virginia, did it ever occur to you that God is doing His best to save your husband?"

And she broke utterly down and sobbed and said: "This is the sixth sweet child I have given up, if he dies, but if God would save my husband I would give them all up, if it should break my heart."

I went down town and hunted her husband up. I met him on the sidewalk and walked up to him, and I slapped him on the shoulder, and said I: "John, I am just from your house, old fellow. And you've just got almost an angel for a wife, and that woman is bathing that sweet, sick child of yours with her tears this moment, and I said to your wife, 'Virginia, do you reckon God is doing His best to save your husband?' and she just sobbed aloud and said: 'If God can save my husband by taking my sweet children from me, He can have them all.' And," said I, "John, in the name of God, surrender and give your heart to God and be religious."

I want to say to you, that man is an earnest, faithful, efficient member of one of the churches in our town, and walking arm in arm with his wife to the church.

Oh, I am so glad that God will not suffer us to perish until He has done His best to save us.

If a man had asked me fifteen years ago—fourteen years and three months ago—if a man had asked me, "My friend, what is the worst thing that could happen to you?" I reckon I would have just spoken up involuntarily and said: "The death of my precious father. Oh, I'd rather lose all than him! And yet my father came to death's door and the providence of God brought me around his dying pillow, and I watched him as he passed out of this world, and I want to say to you this, that God Almighty put my father's corpse

144

in my pathway and I turned around and I said, "I will go back! I will go back!"

And many a time a man has traveled so far that God can never stop him until he has to put his dead wife in his pathway, and many a man has turned around and said, "I will go back! I will go back!" Many a time God has thrown the sweet angel babe, like a sweet angel chiseled out of marble, in the pathway of the father, and stopped him. This much I know: God will never suffer any man to be damned until He has done His best to save him.

I just want to look at every man who has a good religious wife. I want to say this to you, and may the Holy Spirit of God burn it into your conscience. Listen to me, friend! Listen! The man who stamps a good wife's heart and almost crushes the last drop of blood out of it, let me say to you, sir, you owe that wife a debt that you can never pay her until you pay it at the cross of Jesus Christ! You owe those innocent children that throw their arms around your neck and love you with all their heart, you owe those precious, innocent children a debt that you never can pay until you pay it with your wife around the consecrated altar of God.

I had at my home a precious child when I was a wicked, wayward, godless man. It is the only sweet child I ever had that ever looked in my face when I was a wicked, wayward, godless man. That child is in heaven, but, thank God, I have not a single child that looked in its father's face when he was not trying to serve God and do right.

The saddest picture in this world is to see a good wife and good mother do all she can to train her children right and lead her children to heaven, and the husband, by his example and by his life, doing all he can to undo the work of the wife and to curse his children. I have thought many a time, if there is a deeper, darker, more awful place in hell for one than for another, it must be for that husband and that father who, in spite of wife's prayers and children following her example, broke through it all and despised it all and made his bed in hell.

Oh, friends, when you talk about children, if you cannot touch a man when you bring to bear the relation of his precious children, then he is dead to everything that is noble and true and good.

God is going to take something from us. As I said just now, there is many a happy circle in this town—and the Lord has let us go on through other means. Now, you mark what I say at this moment. You had better look out! God don't like the way you are doing, brother. He don't like the example you are setting your children; and if God takes two or three of your sweet children to heaven this winter, you are going to be a better father to those that are left. Now, mark what I tell you!

In a meeting once like this, I threw it open for talking, and one gentleman stood up in the congregation. Said he: "I am from a distant city; I am a stranger to you all, but I love God, and I want to be a Christian all my days, but I want to say some things to fathers. I want you to hear me. I went through the last war and I never went into a battle—and I was in forty or fifty hard-fought battles—that I didn't go in with a solemn vow that if God would spare me through that battle I would be a Christian. Then, when the battle was over, I would promise God that after I got home from the army I would be a Christian. And God spared me through the whole war, and I came home and only received one slight wound during the war, and when I got home I promised God if I married, I would be

146

a Christian, and then God gave me a good wife, and then I said, 'If we ever have children that need to follow a father's example, then I will be religious.' And in the course of time God blessed us with a sweet little Mary and a sweet little Martha.

"And when Mary was eight years old and Martha six I walked in, and a thousand times, I reckon, I had promised God I would be a Christian; and I walked in home from plantation one day, and wife said to me, 'Husband, little Mary is very sick; she has got a very high fever; she is now scarcely conscious.' I walked into that room, and as soon as my eyes fell upon that child, I said to myself, 'Now, sir, your vows to God. Do you recollect the promises you made?' And the child got worse, and worse, and the next day that precious child died, and over the grave of that child I said I would keep my vows; but I got home and I didn't do it. I kept putting it off till next day. Just a week from that I walked into the room, and wife said, 'Husband, precious little Martha is taken just like little Mary,' and I never went into the house at all—I just went off to the woods and fell down on my knees and said, 'Lord, if you will spare that precious little child I am going to be a Christian right here and now.' And I made my surrender uncompromisingly to God right there.

"I got up off my knees and I went back to the house, and my wife met me on the porch and said, 'Strange to say, husband, the fever is all gone, and the child is getting right peart,' and I said, 'Wife, I am not astonished. I have just got off my knees out yonder in the woods, and I told the Lord if He would spare my child I would be a Christian from this day; and, oh, if I had done that a week ago our precious little Mary would have been with us to-day.' "

Oh, you don't know, brother, how many thousand ways

God has used to bring you to a better and nobler life. I know there are people that will laugh and people that will ridicule the very thought that I am on; but I believe in the providence of God as strong as I believe in my existence. I believe that God rules in this world yet and that the very hairs of my head are numbered and that God does not allow the sparrow that chirps in the thicket to fall to the ground until He has signed its death warrant.

God knows me and knows my children, and He knows best. I have said to God on my knees: "God, you know best what is needed for my soul. If anything in the ordinary means of grace won't save me, God, use extraordinary means on me; whatever in thy wisdom will bring me closer to thee, gracious Father, let those means be used on me!"

Can you feel that way? Many a time I have gone home—and if there ever was any fellow that loved home I reckon I do—and thought of this persistent effort I was making here in St. Louis, leaving all I had to come and help you—left everything in the world—loving wife that I loved, anything—to come here and help you in this meeting; and I want to say to you, brethren and friends, whatever is best for me, whatever is best for my children and for my home, my God, may that come upon us. If it is poverty, I would rather starve to death in one poor hovel, if that means getting to heaven, than have wealth and ride in purple and fine linen, and be damned at last. Nothing in this world will pay me for going to hell, and I say, Lord God, let anything come but that!

God calls us by His providence. I believe in the providence of God, cannot help believing it. And God not only calls us by His providence, not only by His ministry, but as Mr. Spurgeon once said, "God calls us in a thousand ways if we would just stop and listen. Why," said he, "when we walk out in the morning, God makes His sun preach to us. As the sun climbs the slippery steeps of the skies God makes him whisper down to us: 'Oh, man, look at my pathway, upward and onward, brighter and brighter! How is your pathway?' And when the sun poises himself at meridian, he says: 'Man, I have gone half of my day's journey. Have you?' And as he descends toward the west, he says: 'Man, I am going down behind the western hills, and you are going down to the grave.' And when he sinks behind the western hills, he says: 'Man, will you go down with me to-day and paint the splendors of your life over the horizon of your death, or will you go down to a cloudy, fearful, dark, hopeless abyss?' "

And when we walk into our family room at night and light the gas, the little candle-fly flits around, and we brush it off and say, "Foolish thing, don't burn yourself to death," and then the little fly, the little mote, flies around the light and darts into it and burns itself to death, and God makes the little dead mote speak and say, "Man, you are doing the very same thing. You are dazzled by the pleasures and appearance of life, and you have already scorched your immortality, and you are darting down into an eternal and everlasting despair."

When you come to your table and sit down and there are the children gathered around you, and you help their plates, God says, "As you are willing to give food and raiment to your children around you, man, come to me. I am more willing to give you good things than you are to give food to your children."

As you go into your room at night and shut the door, God says, "So, man, heaven's door is going to be shut some of these days. Will you be on the outside or will you be inside forever?"

And when some sudden move awakens you at night, then God says: "Be ye also ready, for ye know not the day or hour when the Son of man cometh."

Are you a farmer? Every time you go out in your field to sow seed, God says: "Man, I have been sowing the seed of life in your heart all your days." When you come out to look at the grain growing so beautifully, God says: "Man, where are those seeds I have sown in your heart?" When you go out to reap your wheat, God says: "Man, the sickle of death will reap you down after a while." When you thrash it and separate the wheat from the chaff, God says: "Man, that is just where I shall be by and by, separating the wheat from the chaff, and the chaff shall be burned with unquenchable fire."

Are you a lawyer? Every time a client comes to you, God whispers back and says: "Man, have you an advocate up yonder to plead your cause before the eternal bar of God?"

Are you a school teacher? Jesus says: "Learn of me, for I am meek and lowly in heart."

Are you a blacksmith? Every time you bring your hammer down on the anvil, God says: "Oh, man, I have been hammering your heart with the hammer of my word and love all your days, and yet it will not give."

Are you a merchant? Every time you measure off a yard of calico God says: "Man, I am measuring off your days to you." And when you take the scissors and clip the cloth, God says, "Man, the scissors of death will cut you loose from time some of these days." As you put your sugar in the scales and weigh it, God says: "Mene, mene, tekel; you are weighed in the balance and found wanting."

As I turn my eyes to the burning fire in the grate at

150

night, God says: "Man, will you shun that fire that shall never be extinguished?"

As the grand old Mississippi floats by, God says: "Man, will you flow over on the banks of the River of Life, and drink its water forever?"

And as you look out upon the shade trees of this city, God says, "Man, will you eat of the fruit of life, and sit down under the tree of life in the world above up yonder?"

As you look at the stars above your head, God whispers back and says, "I have sprinkled the canopy of this moral universe with golden promises, and I bid you look up and live."

As I look at the sun, the sun says, "I will grow dim, but you shall live on." As I look at the moon, the moon says, "I shall sink in darkness and be turned to blood, but your immortal spirit shall live in heaven forever, or be with the damned outcast."

And no matter who I am, or where I am, or what I am doing, God is calling me every minute to a noble and better life.

Friends, will you hear these calls?

Because I have called and ye have refused—Oh, the numberless calls of God. God not only calls me once, but He has called me a thousand times, and not only called me a thousand times, but ten thousand times.

And then I saw another thing right at this point, and the Holy Spirit of all grace help me to seal these words upon the consciences of those people here: God has not only called you a thousand times, but you have heard every one of those calls. Oh, my brother, you have not only heard them with your ears, but those calls have been ringing down through the chambers of your soul and you have

151

heard them down to the innermost depths of your conscience. You have heard all the calls of God.

And God has not only called you ten thousand times, and you have not only heard all those calls, but—most awful point of all—you have understood those calls. You knew what they meant. But there is something else at hand, something else you wanted to look to, something else you wanted to attend to; and now, my brother, after God has called us one thousand times, and we have heard all those calls, and we have understood all those calls, then, if we perish, we perish awfully, and we perish eternally! Oh, just think a moment! Oh, how many calls! How many calls!

Because I have called, and ye have refused; I have stretched out my hands, and no man regarded. Oh, when I think that God has not only called us, but is stretching out His merciful hand and saying: "Here, take it! take it! Whoever will, let him take the water of life freely"; and of how He has stooped down from heaven and pushed His divine hand out in reach of every man in the world and said: "Whoever will, let him take that which I am offering to him," I am lost in love and praise.

You see that mother yonder. She is calling little Willie, and little Willie turns his head and hears mama calling and he runs on, and mama calls little Willie, and he pays no attention to her voice, and directly little Willie looks back at mama and mama has stretched out her arms to him, and those arms have always been resistless to him, and he has always run to them when they were stretched out. And if you just look up and listen to the voice of God, you may see His great loving arms outstretched over you! Oh, how true this is. "I have stretched out my hand and no man regarded."

Now: "I will laugh at your calamity, and mock when your fear cometh." Brethren, I announce the most fearful truth this moment in the moral universe of God. Hear it. I see men laughing to-day and scoffing to-day and reviling to-day and despising to-day. Listen! The most fearful announcement in the book of God is this: "What measure ye mete shall be measured to you again."

Your time is now spent in laughing and scoffing and despising. Just the way you treat God now He will treat you by and by. "What measure ye mete shall be measured to you again." Good measure, heaped up, shaken down and running over! Oh, brother, as you laugh at the pleading, earnest face of God, just so, the book says, God "will laugh at your calamity and mock when your fear cometh."

Oh, sirs, now you have got me at a point in the moral thought of this world that I do not understand. "God laughing at the calamity of a soul! God laughing at my calamity! Do you mean that?" Then I ask you this question —while God in His divine love and compassion calls you, I will ask you one question:

Do you laugh at God? Do you? As God stretches out His hands and begs and pleads, will you, can you, laugh? Do you laugh at God? Will you explain that? Then, if you will, I will explain to you how God "will laugh at your calamity and mock when your fear cometh."

I tell you how I'm going to do it, God helping me. I am going to treat God to-night just like I want Him to treat me when I am helpless and powerless at the judgment bar. As I look at the loving, gentle face of God, and He yearns in heart and soul for me now, I return that yearning to God and say, "My God and my Father, I hear thee, I will obey thee." And then, by and by, when I call upon God, when I lift my voice at the judgment, I will say:

153

"Jesus, lover of my soul,
    Let me to thy bosom fly,
While the nearer waters roll,
    While the tempest still is high.

"Hide me, O my Saviour, hide,
    Till the storm of life be past;
Safe into the haven guide,
    Oh, receive my soul at last.

"Other refuge have I none,
    Hangs my helpless soul on thee; . . ."

And Jesus will say, "Inasmuch as I called you yonder and you answered not, when you call on me I will answer: 'The measure ye mete shall be measured to you again.'"

And, brother, I am going to heed God and He will heed me by and by.

Now, I say I can't explain the text! I don't know its depth, but I will say this: A preacher some time ago gave me the finest illustration of what this text means that I ever found or heard of before.

He said in the town where he was pastor there lived out about two miles in the country a wealthy gentleman—a very wealthy man, and a good man, too. He said that gentleman had only one child, a son, and he said that gentleman just lavished all his kindness and generosity and wealth upon that boy, that was the pride of his father's heart. His father sent him to college and lavished everything in the educational line upon him that could be given him. When that boy returned from college, instead of an educated, refined gentleman, he returned a drunken sot. And his father lavished every kindness that the human heart could conceive upon that drunken, wayward boy. The boy went from bad to worse; and, the preacher said,

"I have looked at his father and I thought to myself, 'That boy is literally stabbing his father to death.' "

Oh, me! There is the way to kill a mother or a father without any weapon. The father of two or three drunken boys said to me, "Jones, my boys are killing their mother, my precious wife. What can I do? What would you do? It don't look like their mother will live twelve months longer."

"Well," said I, "I don't know, brother, I declare! You puzzle me with that question, but I'll say this much. If I ever raise a boy at my house that is a drunken debauchee, and my boys turn out to be drunken vagabonds, and just crush their mother's heart with it, some night or morning after they wake up sober, I'm going to call them into their room, and say, 'Boys, you are killing your precious mother by the inch. She is dying a hundred deaths! Boys, listen to me: Go up in your room and get the old breach-loading shotgun, and put forty buckshot into each barrel, and walk down to the breakfast table this morning, and put it to your mother's head and fire both barrels. You shan't kill my precious wife by inches. You may bring your shotgun and shoot her down, but you shan't kill her by inches that way, boys.' "

Oh, me! There's many a precious woman in this town who is dying by the inch, and you can run home to-night and put your ear to her heart and hear the blood drip! drip! drip! May God have mercy upon us.

That boy went on from bad to worse, until one day, the preacher told me, the father drove into town one morning; got out of his buggy and started down the sidewalk and met this drunken boy. And this drunken boy, in his rage from liquor, took hold of his father and cursed him and handled him rudely and mistreated him. He said the father turned right round and went back and got in his buggy and drove off toward home. And he was watched; they could see from his face that there had been an awful change in that father's mind and heart. And that father drove up in the grove in front of his house and hitched his horse and walked down to the far edge of the grove, and when he reached the farthest point from the house he was seen to put his hands above his head this way (here Jones clasped his hands on the top of his head), and gave the most awful screams that ever escaped human lips. He took his hands down and then placed his hand above his head again and a wail of infinite despair as loud almost as human voice could be pitched escaped his lips, and then he threw his hands up one more time, and such another wail scarcely ever greeted the ear of human being, and then he turned calmly round and walked back to his house. And in about half an hour, he said, this drunken boy came staggering up on the steps, and the father met him on the front porch and turned him deliberately round and said: "Off these premises forever! You are no longer anything to me. I have cut loose from you forever!"

And he drove that boy off his premises.

And ten days from that, that poor, miserable boy died in the gutter in that town, and his father never went near him, never attended his funeral, never paid any more attention than if he had been a stranger in a strange land.

Listen to me, friend! I know if Jesus Christ ever did His best anywhere, it was in Jerusalem. If there was a spot on earth that Christ loved, it was Jerusalem. If there was a people He had longed for and prayed over, it was the people of Jerusalem. And listen! As He looked over the doomed city, He said, "Oh, Jerusalem! Jerusalem! Jerusalem! How oft would I have gathered thee under my wings as a hen gathereth her chickens, but ye would not. Now, behold, your house is left unto you desolate."

Oh, the soul that God tells good-by is gone forever. The soul that God shall speak to in language like this:

> Ye shall seek and shall not find me.
> Ye shall die in your sins.

God has spoken it and God shall never retract His word in time or eternity.

The Lord God have mercy upon us and, whatever else we do, help us to attend to the salvation of our souls, and hear and obey His calls. Will you, to-night?

If I had a thousand tongues they would all talk for Christ; a thousand hands, they would all work for Christ; a thousand feet, I'd put them all on the road to heaven.

S. J.

8. CONSECRATION

Now let us be prayerful while we consider different phases of the subject of consecration.

I beseech you, therefore, brethren, by the mercies of God, that ye present your bodies a living sacrifice, holy, acceptable unto God, which is your reasonable service.

And be not conformed to this world, but be ye transformed by the renewing of your mind, that ye may prove what is that good and acceptable and perfect will of God.

For I say, through the grace given unto me, to every man that is among you not to think of himself more highly than he ought to think, but to think according as God soberly, dealt to every man the measure of faith.

As we look around us in the Christian world, brethren, we are forced to admit that there is such a thing as graduated Christianity, that there are such things as grades among the people of God. What a difference there is between people with the same hopes and the same fears, who are bending their steps to the same judgment, accountable alike to God for vain and idle thoughts, and every word they say. What a difference! Did you ever think about it? That man sitting back there says, "My wife is better than I am. She is a good Christian. I am not much of a Christian." That boy says, "Mother is the best woman

I ever saw. I belong to the same church she does, but I am not much of a Christian." I do wonder if there is such a thing in the kingdom of Christ as the Lord demanding that some of us shall do our best while others are let off very easily. I wonder if my Father in heaven wanted my mother to be a better Christian than He wants me to be. I wonder if in the arrangement of His divine plan He fixed it so that my mother could be a whole Christian and me only a piece of one. I have thought about these things. I have thought whether the kingdom of Christ reserved for my father privileges which helped to make him a magnificent Christian, while I, his son, have none of those privileges and can enjoy none of those privileges.

In regard to this, I often think of the good old brother in the Quarterly Conference in our State. It was the first Quarterly Conference of the year, and the new preacher had been in only two or three weeks. The presiding elder presided, and when the question came up, "How much has been raised during the present quarter for the support of the minister?" one member got up and reported from his church, and another from his, and directly a good old brother stood up and said: "Well, I have been wanting to see the preacher, and see how many children he had, because we want to arrange matters just as economically as we can. It is a hard time among us, and up to this time I have not raised anything." The Presiding Elder glared at the old brother and said: "Brother, you say you have not raised a cent?"

"No, sir, not a cent up to this time," was the reply.

"Well," said he, "how would you have it more economical than that? You have raised nothing up to this time."

And I have many a time, in looking at some people who do not want their religion to be in their way, who do not want it to become burdensome to them, who do not want their religion to affect their reserved rights, and all that sort of thing—I have looked at them many a time and thought, how would you have your religion looser than it is? What more privileges would you ask than you have? I tell you, every slack-twisted, one-horse, no-account member of the church is a positive damage to the church. He lowers the standard, and would let down the kingdom and patience of Jesus to a plane where it is hardly possible to distinguish between a man in the church and one out of the church.

We are getting the thing down now to where we are somewhat like the preacher in Georgia who, when he held his Church Conference and called the list of the members, had the members answer for themselves when they were present, and when they were absent somebody represented them. And he called the name of an absent brother and the preacher said: "Well, how about this brother who is away? Where does he live? What sort of a man is he?" One brother said: "I know the man. He does not go to church as much as he might, but he is a good, clever man." Another brother got up and said about the same, and directly another brother got up and said: "I live close by the man. He is a close neighbor of mine. Although it is true he does not do his whole duty, he is a mighty good man, and there is only one thing that can be said against him, and that is he is a little inclined to be quarrelsome when he is drunk." That was the only difficulty with him.

How often we hear it said: "She is a mighty good woman, but she goes to the theater." "They are mighty pious people, they are, but they play cards every night." "They are very good people, and there is only one thing to be said against them, and that is that they dance." Oh, how

161

we are letting down, down, down! The fact is, we have let the church down so low that you cannot ditch her off. There is not fall enough to ditch her, and we are getting into a sad fix when that is the case. A good lady told me this morning: "There is a heap of people never lived in the country, and they do not understand your illustrations." I am not responsible for your ignorance. They are very plain to me. We have got down too low, that is the idea.

Now, I suppose we have in all the churches about three grades of Christians. In our blue Masonic lodges we have what we call entered apprentice Masons, fellow-craft Masons, and master Masons. Those are the three grades in the blue lodge. Some will stop at the entered apprentice degree and never go any further, and they are called entered apprentices. Others pass to the fellow-craft degree and stop there, and then they are what we denominate fellow-craft Masons. Others rise to the sublime degree of master Masons, and they are called master Masons. I might say that we have three classes of Christians in our churches: our entered apprentice Christian, our fellow-craft Christian, and our master Christian.

The entered apprentice Christian, he is the little fellow out there that made profession and joined the church, and that is all he has ever done, and that is all he is ever going to do. That is the end of it with him. I used to get out of patience with these people. If you want them to do anything they will say: "I never was called upon to do that," and they would not advance and get religion right. They will say, "Oh, I am a member of the church," and then get on the other side of the fence and remain there.

To me they seem like an old ox in a hot, dry lane, and he just lives in that lane, with the beautiful green pastures on both sides of the road, and all the grass the poor old fellow gets he bites through the fence, and he gets his nose rubbed sore by always biting through the fence. I am always sorry for those old oxen. And there is many a Christian in the lane, between Chenot and the world, you know. They won't go over into the green pastures of God's love, and they won't go over into the valley on the devil's side. They are what you might call starvelings in the land, and they are numerous, too.

The entered apprentice Christian: "Oh, I have made a profession of religion. I have been baptized." And that is all they seem to know, and all they want to know about Christianity at all. The Lord forgive us if we have ever had such low, groveling ideas of Christianity as that. Why, brother, just think a moment. Suppose that all there was in Christianity to you, my brother, or you suppose that all there was in it, was the simple fact that you had made profession and joined the church, and that was the end of the whole matter. Suppose it was. I declare to you that if that was all there was in it, here is one brother who would hush his mouth and never try to make another convert to Christianity. I would do that if Christianity was simply joining the church and making a profession of religion.

The entered apprentice Christians: They are the little fellows in the church. I was sitting on a car one day, and when the conductor came round and took up the tickets there were eight or ten passengers whom he never asked for any tickets. He let them go free. They were the little fellows, two and three and four years old. He never bothered them at all. And, I think, in the Church of God we ought to pass these little fellows and not make them pay a cent. Just let them go free. The only way you little fellows can get to heaven is by hanging on the skirt of some good old mother and making out that you are one of her little children. I do not know how else you are to get in.

There is a little fellow just twelve months old. He never walked a step, and you know it. He cannot understand when you tell him anything. He is mentally and physically incapacitated from being of service to you. And those little fellows in the church, they only join the church and make a profession of religion. They have not the physical, or at least the intellectual, ability to be of any account in the church.

Now, I grant that it is a grand effort in a man's life when he gives his life to God and joins the ranks of Christ. Oh, that is grand! But suppose every soldier in the last war had gone and registered his name as a soldier and sworn allegiance to the Southern Confederacy, and then turned round and gone back home. He would have met the other forces with a vengeance, would he not? And when we go up and put our name down on God's side, and swear allegiance to His cause, and then go on about our business and say: "That is all there is to it," it is just a question of census. We can just tell how many there are in the family and give their names. That is all there is in Christianity. Just barely the taking of the census.

The entered-apprenticeship Christian. A number of them got mad with me once because I said that if I got an order for one hundred of them I would not ship them by freight or express, but I would put them in a paper box and put a two-cent stamp on it and send them off that way —these little entered-apprentice fellows. It would be foolish to make them into a twenty-five-cent package when you could send them O. K. anywhere for two cents. But I reckon I shall never get an order for any of that sort. I never heard of any of them being of any account in heaven or earth.

The entered-apprentice degree comes before the fellow-craft degree. You must take that step first—profess Christ and openly and publicly join the church. That is the right step. But do not let that be the end, let that be a step to something higher. Well, the next step is the fellow-craft degree, and the fellow-craft Christians have not only joined the church and made an open and public profession of religion, but they will do some things very readily and willingly when you want them to be done. If you want them to pay, why they will pull out their pocketbook and divide the last dollar with you. That is good, too. I like to see a liberal man. In fact, I have no patience with any except a liberal man. I never saw a Christian succeed in doing much that was a downright stingy man. Now we have what we call fellow-craft Christians that have made profession of religion and joined the church. They will pay every time you ask them, but if you say, "Brother, let us hear you pray," they say, "I never pray in public." They have reserved rights and no man ever made a good Christian who had reserved rights. "Some things I will do, some I won't." The fellow-craft Christians, when they feel like it, will do anything you ask them to do, but if they don't feel like it they won't touch it. Well, if a fellow has no brains he ought to let his emotional nature direct him. That is my judgment. If a fellow has no intellectual nature, then his emotional nature ought to run him, and he ought to keep red hot all the time. But if I have any brains at all I am never going to let my feelings run me.

When our child cries with pain it puts its hand on its pain and we hear and heed it, and I reckon that when the Lord's people cry they can put their hand on their pain and cry. And a great many of His little children are crying from the fact that they will be damned. That is about as low a ground as you can afford to stand on. Some of us are crying, "Lord, I want to get to heaven." That is the object. They say, "I will take care of myself here if the Lord will take care of me when I die." "Oh, if I can just get to heaven when I die I will be the happiest person that ever lived on the face of this earth." They are fellow-craft Christians. They will do anything in the world if they feel like it. I have known Brother A to be called upon to pray at a big revival meeting, and he would pray earnestly in a big, loud voice. But let him cool off a little and he won't pray for his life. He must be excused. I never did understand that a good Christian could do at one time what he could not do at another. I never could understand a man that would grow beautifully less all the time. I thought that as Christianity was developed, it grew larger and stronger.

Feeling! Sister, I run on this idea. If a thing is right I'll do it, and I will never stop to ask whether I feel like it or not. "I'll do it if I feel like it. If I don't, I won't." The most efficient sermons I ever preached were when I felt least like preaching. God blesses us not by the success of our efforts or by the spirit of buoyancy that actuates us, but by the efforts we put forth whether we feel like it or not.

A woman's child is sick. The mother never stops to see whether her own head aches or not, whether she has rheumatism or not. But she looks at the interest of that child and cares for it. And so every Christian person ought to look and see what the claims of God are upon him. You can tell the fellow-craft Christian in this way: If it is a right pretty Wednesday night he is out at prayer meeting. If it is sort of dark or misty or rainy, he won't come out; he is afraid he will take cold. There are a great many peo-

166

ple in this world who have an idea that a church is the most unhealthy place in the world. "Why," they say, "I took cold there one day and did not get over it in six weeks." Look here, I have been going to church two and three times a day for years, and did you ever see a fatter, healthier looking man in your life than I am? I tell you it is not churchgoing that makes folks sick. That ain't it. "If it is pleasant and everything works all right I will go." Or, to put it in a sensible, solemn, serious way, if you would rather have it, here is a man physically afraid to go to church. Here is a man going to church three or four times a day, and I am a stronger man physically than I have been in fifteen years.

The fellow-craft Christian: If everything is fair he is there. If there is anything in the way he is absent. "If it is convenient to have family prayers we will have them." "If it is right convenient to go to prayer-meeting we will go, but if it ain't we won't." Don't you see how we can make our religion bend to it as fellow-craft Christians? Well, I am tired of talking about this sort of Christians in the world. But a fellow must be a fellow-craft Christian as he must be an entered-apprentice Christian. I would want to be an entered-apprentice Christian about sixty seconds, and a fellow-craft Christian about thirty minutes, and a master Christian forever and ever. A master Christian, forever and ever!

What constitutes a master Christian? He is one who has presented his body as a living sacrifice, holy, acceptable unto God, which is his reasonable service. He is one who has not conformed to this world in any way, but has transformed himself by renewing his mind. He is one who thinks soberly and wisely on all things; he loves God with all his heart, and loves his neighbor as himself.

Master Christians! Oh, brethren and sisters, they are worth their weight in gold to any community in the world. They are worthy to be cherished. They will do what they promise to do. They are living to God and to duty and to every good word and work.

The master Christian! Now, let me tell you. The entered-apprentice Christian, as an entered-apprentice Christian, can never be a master Christian. A fellow-craft Christian, as a fellow-craft Christian, can never be a master Christian. The master Christian, thank God Almighty, can never, and will never, be satisfied on any lower plane than that which God and Christ raise.

Now, I wish we could take this twelfth chapter of Romans and read it through. There is not a verse in it but that ties right along onto the discussion. There is room in there for all of your thought and all your will and all your muscles and all your desires. If you take that twelfth chapter of Romans, which is practically a plain setting-forth of Christian duty, march out in this character and look for Jesus, the author and finisher of our faith.

I was once preaching in a town of 1,200 or 1,500 inhabitants, and there had long been a family feud there, and it had involved nearly all the family connections. It went from bad to worse, until pistols were used and until the thing had gotten into the most corrupt shape. Now, one of the principal parties was a widow, whose heart and life and children were involved in this fearful difficulty. When I finished preaching—and the first time, I reckon, for months and years that both parties were in God's house at one time—the meeting was thrown open for talk. One talked and then another talked, and directly this woman stood up about the middle of the house. She looked at me with a flush on her face and a sparkle in her eye, and she was one of the most intelligent looking women I ever met; she looked at me and dropped her finger on me and said: "Sir, if there is a woman on God's earth who has literally lived in a fire for years I am that woman. I was once a happy child of God, and how unutterably miserable I have been. Listen to me, sir, and I record the words before the judgment bar of God and before mankind. If crucifying myself and denying myself and giving up all that God despises, loving my enemies, doing good to those that despitefully use me—if that will take a soul to salvation I am just as good for salvation as if I had stepped inside the golden gates."

Then she stepped across the house, and, taking the hand of her enemy, she said: "To-day I bury many fathoms below the surface of the earth every unkind thought, word, and act of my life. From this moment what I do shall be by the faith of the Son of God that loved me and gave His life for me."

I returned and saw that woman twelve months after that, and she said: "Blessed be God! Twelve months of my way to the good world have passed without a disturbing ripple or a darkening cloud."

Twelve months later I met her again, and she said: "Not a cloud, not a difficulty. Just swept right along to the good world, and if you get there yourself you may look out for me; I am going through."

Oh, the soul that settles all these questions, that will deny and crucify himself, that will give up the world and all that God despises, and trusts in Jesus, can say: "That will take me to heaven; I am just as good for heaven as if I was there."

What a consecration it is to put all you have got in God's bank and say: "Now, Lord, there it is, use it! Use it to thy glory," and then turning round to this old world, say, "All I have got is in God Almighty's bank, and if that bank don't break I am a millionaire forever. I will trust all I have in the hands of God." That is the sort of Christianity we want.

But you say: "I have for months and years listened to the voice of God, and may He direct me, but sometimes the voice of the world has been so loud that I admit my ear has been turned to hear what the world has to say. God forgive me, I will not do it any more." Listen only to God. You cannot get into grander and deeper water. Let us say now: "I will never listen to the old world any more. I will listen only to Christ."

I want to say to you that there is a great harvest in store for us if the Lord can only get us in time where He can pour down His Spirit upon us. I tell you another thing, the reason I know Christianity is divine. If Grover Cleveland had gone through the United States denouncing the Democratic party and the members of the party as I have denounced members of the church and professors of religion in this town, he would have broken his party all to pieces. But you attack religion, and the more fuel you put around the fire, the more it burns, and the more there is left. Oh, for a pure Christianity, and may it permeate this whole city! Oh, give us the sacred apostolic Christianity that counts all things as loss but for the excellency of the knowledge of Christ Jesus our Lord. Let us work as if we were hired to work our way to heaven. Let us trust Jesus as if we could not work without Him, and God will bathe us in the spirit of Christianity and bless us for it our entire life.

Oh, Lord! Teach men that while God Almighty runs His trains at our feet every day, and checks up enough for all of us to get aboard, it is the bounden duty of every man to step on board and go to God and glory.

S. J.

9. HOW CAN YOU BE SAVED?

We invite your prayerful attention to these words:

What must I do to be saved? And they said: Believe on the Lord Jesus Christ and thou shalt be saved, and thy house.

As a minister of the Gospel of Christ I have no right to advise a man to do anything that he cannot die doing and die saved. When that question is propounded to me as a minister of the Gospel, I cannot answer it in any way except the scriptural way. As a minister, I have no right to advise a man to do anything in order that he may be saved unless I am conscious the advice given will surely bring about salvation to him.

Now, I might advise a man to pray in his family—and every father ought to pray with the children of his home. I cannot see how any man who loves his children, and believes that his children are immortal, can let morning and night pass by day after day, and no devotion in his home; and yet I see how a man may pray in his family all his life and die unsaved. I might advise a man to read good books —and I know that that is good advice, and I am satisfied that nothing can be more pernicious than bad books, and nothing more helpful than good books—yet I see how a man may read good books all his life and die unsaved. I might advise a man to keep good company—and, above all things, we ought to keep no other sort—and yet I see how a man may keep company with God's people, with good men and women all his life, and die unsaved.

I might advise a man to join the Church of Jesus Christ —and I know that is good advice. I wish every man and woman and boy and girl would join the Church of God to-night and take the vows of the church upon them and live up to those vows. Oh, how much better and brighter this world would be around us! I say, when I advise a man to go into the Church of Jesus Christ, that is good advice. The message of the Church of God to this old world is: "Come thou and go with us and we will do thee good."

And I know I give you good advice when I say to all men, come into the church; it will be healthful to you, it will be like a restraint thrown around you, it may lead you to a nobler, better life.

One of the most remarkable incidents—I now think of it in connection with this thought—one of the best women I remember to have had in my charge as a pastor—true, noble, good Christian woman—said to me one day, "Did you ever hear how it was I got into the church?" Said I, "No." "Well," she said, "I was about a fifteen-year-old girl, and I was standing just outside of my pew in the aisle when the congregation arose to sing, and the preacher opened the door of the church." She said, "I stepped a little out from between the pews and took my stand in the aisle and stood there singing, and a mischievous schoolmate of mine standing behind me gave me a push and started me up the aisle, and started me so forcibly I could not stop, and I just went right on up and gave the preacher my hand, and," she said, "that is how I came in the church."

She said, "I was so impressed by the fact that I did join

the church that it made me very serious, and the following week, whenever wrong or error would come up, I'd say, 'I cannot do that; I am a member of the church,' and that thing so weighed upon me until, finally, I said, 'Can I perpetuate a membership in the church and not be religious?' and I sought the Saviour, and I found Him. And I would not take the world for that push that girl gave me that day."

The fact of the business is, it don't make much difference what starts you, so you get a good start. There's a heap in that.

And I will say another thing. You don't live many blocks from here, and the way is just as plain before your eye from here to your house as it is from where you sit to where these burners are lighted, and yet you could not get to your home to-night without starting, much less to heaven without starting.

I say, I would give you good advice if I were to say to you, "Come into the Church of God," and yet I can see how a man may live and die outside of the Church of God, and be saved. I would say, "Commemorate the sufferings and death of Jesus Christ," and I believe every soul for whom Jesus died ought to commemorate His sufferings and His death around the sacramental board—and yet I see how a man may partake of the sacrament regularly and then go down to hell at last. I might advise a man to be baptized in the name of the Trinity—God said to the ministers, "Go out into the world and preach the gospel to every creature, and tell them they that believe and are baptized shall be saved"—and yet I can see how a man may go from baptism to death and hell. I may advise a man to make a profession of religion and love it, and yet I can see how a man may go from the heights of profession down

175

into the depths of damnation. These are all grand instru-
mentalities in the hands of God, and I would not under-
estimate any one of them—but there is one sufficiency, and
that is faith in the Lord Jesus Christ.

Now, we propose to speak straight through to the text:
"What must I do to be saved?" We'll notice some of these
small words in this text. There is force in each one of
them. This is infinitely the most important question ever
propounded by man—"What must I do to be saved?"

Now, it is not, "What must I think?" It is not, "How
must I feel?" It is not, "Where must I go?" It is, "What
must I do to be saved?"

We get to God through movement. A man cannot think
his way to God. This world, by its wisdom, cannot know
God. A man cannot find God by going to the temple, or on
this mountain. The question is not, "How must I feel?"
or "What must I think?" but it is: "What must I do to be
saved?" . . . "Not every one that sayeth, Lord, Lord, but
he that doeth the will of my Father which is in heaven."

Now, we have got a great deal of mystery mixed up with
what we call religion. Why, if there were not mysteries in
the Bible I'd discard it in a moment; I'd know some trick-
ster wrote it. If I knew every mystery in the word of God,
I'd know some man like myself wrote it. Ingersoll said in
one of his lectures: "The Bible! the Bible! Why," said he,
"I could write a better book myself." Some old woman got
up and said: "You better get at it, there's money in it."
And that is what Ingersoll is after.

I say, there are mysteries there that I can never solve. I
grant you that I never can see with my finite eye how the
God over all could ever be an infant a span long. I can
never understand that. I can never see how the babe in
the manger at Bethlehem can be the King of angels. I can

not solve that problem. I never could understand how the great God who upholds all things could be carried about in Mary's arms. I can never solve that. I never could understand how He that owned the cattle on the thousand hills and implanted the bowels of this earth with gold, how He could send His disciples to the fish's mouth to get money to pay His taxes. These are things I can never solve; but I believe in my heart that Jesus of Nazareth, the carpenter's despised boy, was the King of angels and God's only begotten Son, and the brightest hopes in this world cluster around and bud and blossom out of just such faith as this.

Now, we ministers have adopted a phrase that is delusive in itself—"getting religion." "When did you get religion?" "I got religion so and so." Well, what does a man mean when he says, "I have got religion"? There's nothing in the book about folks getting religion—there's not a word on that subject. You cannot point your finger to a single instance where any man ever said, "I got religion way back yonder, so and so." That term is deceptive in itself. And a great many people think, "When I get religion I will get hold of a huge sentiment that will stir me up from head to foot." Well, religion is not a shout, it is not a song, it is not a sentiment, it is not getting happy, it is not shouting. Shouting, getting happy, is no more a part of religion than my coat is a part of me. I have got a coat, thank God! I couldn't get along well without one; but I would be just as much myself without the coat as I am with one; and, thank God Almighty, I can be just as good and just as religious and just as Christ-like, and never shout, as I can be to shout my way to glory.

We have really mystified this whole subject in our experiences. We have taught men to believe that, somehow or another, religion was something that came down on a man and was thrust into his soul, and that he was a different man altogether in an instant. Many a fellow gets up at meeting and says: "I got it! I got it! I got it right in here!" Well—got what? Now, that is the big question. Got what? And if he don't mind, it will be buried with him right in there; it will never get out. When they bury him, they can say, "Here lies a solid lump; it never evaporates, effervesces, or anything."

What is "getting religion"? What do you mean by that? I notice that when Christ Himself mingled with men, and talked with men face to face, His term was, "Follow me, follow me, go with me somewhere." Not, "Take something and sit down there and enjoy it," but, "Come, take my hand, and go with me somewhere."

Religion is not something that bubbles out of the lips and from the lungs of a man, but motive power taking one somewhere. Or, in other words, when a man says, "I have got religion," I have just got one question to ask him. I mean, sir, this: When Jesus Christ knocked at the door of your heart, did you open the door of your heart and let Christ in, and is He there now? And is the life that you now live by the faith of the Son of God that loved you and gave Himself for you?

Now, I have seen a man get up from an altar and shout and clap his hands together and say: "Glory to God, I got it!" and yet that same man, three months from that time, gave the falsehood to all of the profession he made by an unfaithful lie. Some of the best men I have ever known in my life came to God in the most quiet, unassuming way and they said to me: "I don't know the time or place when God touched me into life, but this much I know, that I live by faith in Christ this moment." "Being made par-

178

taker of the divine nature" is the scriptural term. And what do you mean by that?

This old, dead, dormant, wicked nature of mine has been touched by divine power, and I feel now like I had strength to do what God wanted me to do, and I have now courage to refuse to do the thing that the devil wants me to do, and the world wants me to do. A great part of my life, whenever I had got stirred up, and began to think about who I was, and what I was and where I was going to, the very next thought was: "Well, religion is all a mystery; I don't know anything about it."

A man came up last night and grabbed my hand and said: "I want to be what you said, but I don't know what to be. I don't know anything in the world about it."

Religion is a very plain thing. Do you know that nine-tenths of humanity is very ignorant, and do you think that Jesus Christ would promulgate a religion that nine-tenths of the world would not understand? Do you know that the Lord Jesus Christ would envelop the mysteries of religion in such a fog that the clearest minds would not see into it? He has given us a religion that is so plain that the most ignorant man, though he be a wayfarer, can see through it.

What must I do to be saved? Now, salvation is not a song, as I said just now. It is not sentiment. It is not "getting it"; salvation, if it means anything, means this: Salvation from something and salvation to something; salvation from the wrong and salvation to the right. There is something practical about a thing of that sort. Don't you see? Salvation from profanity and salvation to chastity. Salvation from gambling and salvation toward justice in all my ways. Salvation from the things that degrade me and salvation to the things that ennoble me and elevate me.

179

What is salvation? Well, when you sum it all up, here it is in a nutshell: Salvation is loving everything that God loves, and hating everything that God hates. That is salvation. What a man loves and what a man hates determines his or her character. A good man loves the good and hates the evil. A bad man hates the good and loves the evil. That is the difference. Salvation means being in harmony with the good and out of harmony with the evil, so that you can say, "I love the good and hate the evil."

I am so glad that a man is still considered orthodox among Protestant Christians when he says: "God made me, and I am certain that if God made me God could so alter, vary and change my nature that He could make me love the good and hate the evil, and it is God's own work. Open my eyes, show me the evil, show me the good and make me in answer to my prayer and my surrender to Him to hate the evil and love the good."

Salvation means deliverance from the guilt of sin, deliverance from the love of sin, deliverance from the dominion of sin. Oh, I do not think there is a Protestant book of theology extant that teaches salvation is anything else than deliverance from the guilt of sin, deliverance from the love of sin and from the dominion of sin. I wish we Christian people would live up as high as our books teach us on that subject. I am not a sanctificationist; but I will declare to you, you cannot raise a bigger, higher, deeper howl in the churches of God in this country than to preach about sanctification, than to say that a man can sanctify a man throughout soul and body and spirit, and make him walk arm and arm with God every day. And now people will say, "That man is running off like wildfire now; he has got off on a tangent, and the first thing you know about him he will be in the asylum." That is just about the talk of people who preach on that line. Now, listen, my friend, there is not a plane of Christ where the soul is allowed to sin. The soul is not allowed to sin on the lowest plane, and the only difference between sanctifying a man and regenerating him, as we call it, is the external difference. There is not a particle of external difference. If there is an enemy lurking in the soul, sanctification puts it on the outside. I like that. God knows I have plenty out there to fight, but I do not want any more on the inside. Sanctification puts the last enemy of a man on the outside.

I get up here and preach, "If these sinners do not quit sinning, God will damn them forever." But the church itself has some reserved rights. They say, "Give it to those sinners, but do not say anything about us. Tell them that the Lord will damn them, every one." That is the way we run it off, and other preachers say to those sinners: "The sinner that sinneth shall die in his sin."

What is the message of God to them? "If the righteous man forsake his righteousness and commit iniquity, his righteousness shall be forgotten and he shall die in his sin."

Did you ever read that? And God says to the wicked: "If the wicked man will forsake his wickedness and do right, his wickedness shall not be remembered against him and he shall be saved."

That is the message. Ah, me! There is no better army to fight this world with than an army of Jesus Christ that has been truly saved from sin. I do not want any sentiments or shouting connected with my religion if I can just feel conscious that I am saved from sin. The blood of Jesus Christ cleanseth me from sin.

What must I do to be saved? What can I do to be saved

181

from the guilt, and the life and the dominion of sin? That is the question. What must I do in order to love everything that God loves, and to hate everything that God hates? That is the question.

Well, now, thank God we have an answer, and that answer comes straight to the conscience of every one of us. "Believe in the Lord Jesus Christ, and thou shalt be saved."

Oh, I am so glad that it did not read this way: "Believe the Methodist creed and follow the Methodist discipline and you shall get to heaven."

I am so glad it did not read that way. If it had there is many a man who would have stopped and said: "That I cannot do." I am so glad it did not read: "Believe the Baptist creed and be immersed by the Baptists and follow their precepts and you shall be saved."

I am glad they did not put it that way, for some of us might have objected. I am glad it is not written: "Whosoever believeth the Presbyterian creed and conforms to Presbyterian usages shall be saved."

Some of us might have objected. But, blessed be God, it is not faith in a creed but faith in the Person that saves the soul.

What is a creed? It is nothing but the skin of truth set up and stuffed with something. There is no life in it, no life-giving powers, and no creed *per se* ever saved any man. I am glad we have formulated our doctrines and formulated our creeds. That was necessary, that was right, but, thanks be to God, when I want to be saved—when a poor sinner wants to be saved to God from sin, and saved in heaven—I have nothing to do but fall down at the feet of Jesus Christ and say: "God be merciful to me a sinner." That is it.

Now, there is many a man in heaven that never heard of the Methodist creed. There is many a man in heaven who went there before there was ever a Methodist. Don't you see? There is many a man in the good world who never heard of the Baptist Church. Brethren, don't you bother yourself about this creed or that creed, or try to understand all there may be in any creed, but look yonder

> Hanging on that tree
> In agonies of blood,

And as

> He fixed his languid eyes on——

on you, and you surrender to that divine person on that tree. That is it.

Now, a great many people say that a child is too young to understand the Scriptures; it is too young to join the church. Well, brother, when did you graduate? That is the question. That little ten-year-old boy of yours understands just about as much of the mysteries of redemption as you do. Ain't that so? And our Saviour pushed your sort back, and said: "Suffer little children to come unto me."

And He said something else to you gray-headed gentlemen: "Except ye be converted and become as little children ye shall in no wise enter the kingdom of heaven."

And yonder little child can, blessed be God, take Christ as his Saviour or her Saviour.

This incident I have heard related of Jonathan Edwards, perhaps the greatest man that ever preached the Gospel in America. He heard of the conversion, say, of little Minnie Lee, in a distant state. That good man did not believe that children could know Christ, and he went hundreds of miles to hunt the home of this little girl. And when he rang the front doorbell, or knocked at the door, and was admitted

183

by the mother of the child, he gave her his hand and said: "I am Dr. Edwards. Is this Mistress Lee?" And she bowed and said: "I am Mrs. Lee." "Well," he said, "I have come to talk with your little Minnie." And she said: "Walk into the parlor." He walked in and took a seat. The mother went and dressed little Minnie, combed her hair, and brought her into the parlor looking almost like a little angel. And Dr. Edwards took her on his knee and questioned her and probed and dissected every utterance for almost an hour. Then he took little Minnie and set her in her mother's lap and took out a handkerchief and wiped the big tears from his eyes and said: "Thank God Almighty, a child four years old can have the Lord Jesus Christ."

Oh, brethren, let us bring our children to Christ; let us save them in their younger days. Won't you? Thank God for every agency in this country that brings children to Christ. God bless you, Sunday-school superintendents, and you Sunday-school teachers, and God help you to know Christ yourself, and let the great aim of your lessons at the Sunday-school be to teach your children to come to Christ, a divine person.

"What must I do to be saved?" The answer comes: "Believe on the Lord Jesus Christ and thou shalt be saved."

Wilt thou believe in Christ? I have read a good many books on faith, but I never read one yet that was not as clear as mud. I never read a work on faith that I was not more dissatisfied when I quit reading than I was before I commenced. I have watched authors split a hair a mile long in their efforts to get at the different shades and views and opinions on faith. But I will tell you what faith is.

Steve Holcomb, with his little wharf rats before him at Louisville—a poor little beggar children's Sunday-school—

called four of them out before him and pulled half a dollar out of his pocket and said: "Johnny, you can have that." Johnny sat and looked at it, but never opened his mouth. And he said: "Willie, you may have that," but the little fellow sat and grinned, but never opened his mouth. And he said: "Henry, you may have that," but Henry sat there and never said a word. And he said: "Tommy, you may have that," and Tommy put out his hand, grabbed the money, and ran it down into his pocket.

And Brother Holcomb said: "That is faith."

The other boys cried and cried because they did not take the money. Faith is just taking what God offers you. God offers you Christ and salvation. It is just taking what is offered you, don't you see?

I want to say at this point, brethren, that if a man believes anything after he gets religion that he did not believe before he got religion, I have never got religion. I believe nothing since I got religion that I did not believe before. That is, I never saw a day in my life that I did not believe the Bible. I never saw a line in the Bible in my life that I did not believe. I may be happily constituted, but I want to tell you I believed everything in the Bible, and everything it said about Christ. And I believed He was the Saviour of men. And I believed that twenty-four years ago, when I went within half a mile of eternal perdition. I believe the same thing to-day. But for the last fourteen years, thank God, I have not only believed it, but I have been trying to do it to the best of my ability. I believed it twenty-four years, but went on just like it meant nothing. For fourteen years, thank God Almighty, I have not only believed in Jesus Christ in the sense that I did before, but I have been following Him.

I will tell you what my trouble was. I did not know faith

had its conditions. Now, if I put my hands up that way I cannot see that gas burner to save my life, but if I take my hands down I cannot help seeing it. But when I put my hands up I do not comply with the conditions of sight. When I take them down I do. If I put my hands up I cannot see the gas burner to save my life. Take them down and I cannot help seeing it. Or, if I am riding along the road, and I see an apple on a tree by the side of the road, I say I cannot taste that apple. But a little boy says: "Mister, if you will climb that tree and shake that apple down and bite it you cannot help tasting it." Don't you see that when I am riding along that lane I am not complying with the conditions of taste, but when I stick my teeth in the apple I am?

Now, what are the conditions of faith? I know of but one in this round world, and that is repentance. When a man doesn't repent he can't believe unto salvation to save his life, and if he will repent he can't help from believing, and then he just believes right on. And faith is not an act. Faith is adjusting the soul rightly toward God, and taking what He is willing to give. That's the fact. In other words, faith of the old washwoman that God would send the rain to do her washing—her faith was to ask God for the rain, and tighten every hoop on every tub and push them up under the eaves. There's many a fellow praying for a shower of grace in this country, and all the tubs with every hoop loose and turned bottom side up, and it might rain grace a thousand years, and he'd never catch anything. God Himself can't fill a tub that is bottom side up unless He reverses gravity.

Believe! How may I believe? That's the question. Now, brethren, I bring this down so every man of you can see it, and I aim to be perfectly deliberate, and I aim to be straightforward in this argument. I am trying to put the matter so every one of you can see it, and I want you to see it in the light that God's word teaches it to us—that faith is the attitude of the soul presented toward God, so that he may come and do what he wants to do for us and with us.

And I tell you another thing: The hardest thing a poor fellow ever tried to do in this world is to give himself to God just like he is. He wants to fix up and brush up and arrange the matter. Oh, how bad we do hate to turn just such a case over to God! We would like to make him about half way what we want him to be before we turn him over. It is the hardest job a man ever undertook to turn himself over to God just like he is, just like I am.

I have often thought of that moral, upright boy that was convicted of sin at the camp-meeting and at the same time his servant boy that drove him about was converted. The servant boy went off to the woods and knelt down and gave his heart to God in an hour and was converted, and this boy sought religion all during the camp-meeting at the altar and had them all praying for him. He went home and prayed for two or three weeks and still was not converted, and one day this colored boy came along by his door, and the boy called him in and said: "Harry, look here. I want to understand how it is. You have been the worst boy in this town and you were converted at the same camp-meeting that I was, and you went down in the woods and got religion and gave yourself to God in an hour, and here I've been praying and trying, and I am still in darkness. I know you've got it, but here I've been a moral, upright boy all my life, and I don't know why God will pardon a mean Negro like you are, and here I am, can't get either religion or pardon."

"Well, Marse Henry," says the boy, "I can explain that. As soon as the Lord gave me the spirit of religion I saw myself all in dirty rags, and that moment I went out in the woods and shucked off my dirty rags and said, 'Oh, Lord, clothe me in garments of righteousness,' and the Lord gave them to me right there. But, Marse Henry, you've been a good boy all your life, and you've only got a splotch of mud on clothes, and you've been trying to brush it off for about three weeks, but if you'll only shuck them off and pray the Lord to clothe you in garments of righteousness, He'll do it right there."

And when the boy walked out, the young man fell on his knees and prayed: "God be merciful to me a sinner." And it wasn't long before he was able to say to his driver boy: "Harry, I've got it. I've got it, blessed be God. You taught me a great truth—that I've got to come to God just like I am; no brushing off the mud, and no fixing up about it, but asking God to give me garments brushed for all eternity."

And God Almighty can take the meanest, most abject, wicked sinner and in five minutes He can make the most gentlemanly, clever, kind-hearted fellow out of him that you ever saw in your life.

A man who had been seeking religion for a number of years sent finally for the preacher. The preacher told me this himself, and when he got there this man said: "I have been seeking religion, more or less, for twenty years, and I'm afraid I'll die at last without it, and I've heard of you and I've sent for you to come and tell me what to do."

The brother looked at him and said: "Submit to God."

"Well," he said, "what do you mean by submitting to God?"

The preacher said, "Will you let me baptize you in the name of the Triune God?"

"No," said the man, "I never can do that. I can never be baptized, wicked as I am. That would be wrong."

"Well," said the preacher, "if you won't take the medicine, I'll go. I won't fool with a patient who won't take the prescription."

"Well," said the man, "if you think I ought to be, I will."

"That ain't the question. Will you let me baptize you in the name of the Trinity? Will you submit to the ordinances of God?"

"If you think I ought to be, I will."

"Now," said the preacher, "will you let me administer the sacrament."

"Oh," the man answered, "that would be sacrilege for me to take the sacrament. I can't do that."

"The question is, will you submit to the sacrament of God, sir?"

"I can't do that. I never can do that."

"Well, then, there's no use in me talking to you. You won't take my prescription, and I can't cure you."

Finally, the man said: "If you think I ought to be baptized and ought to take the sacrament, I'll do it."

"Now," said the preacher, "let me receive you into the church."

"Oh, no, a man ought never to join the church until he gets religion. I can't do that."

"Well," said the preacher, "there's no use in bandying words at all."

"Well," said the fellow, "if you think I ought, I will."

The preacher said: "Now, get down, sir, we will pray over this matter."

He got down on his knees and prayed devoutly, and when the preacher arose from his knees, the man, still on his knees, said, "Thank God, I see it now. I'm a saved man."

It is submission to God that is religion. It is walking up and stacking your old gun right at the foot of the cross, taking off your cartridge box and up with your hands: "Good Lord, I'm a surrendered rebel, right here. I'll die before I'll ever touch that old musket again, and I'll never take up that cartridge box again. I've fired my last shot on the devil's side, and now, Lord, I'm a surrendered rebel." You give all to the Lord, and He'll meet you and bring you safe in His arms before any devil in hell can get to you. Surrender! submission!

What must I do to be saved? Believe on the Lord Jesus Christ. Believe on Him, not believe Him. Simply believe on him. Now, I believe Bancroft when he writes a history of the United States—I believe every word he says, but I don't believe on Bancroft. He's of a different party from me, and I don't know that I want to run with him much. And I may believe Benedict Arnold when he writes a history of the American Revolution—believe every word he writes—but I don't believe on Benedict Arnold. He was a traitor, and I don't take any stock in such. But I believe George Washington when he makes a statement, and I not only believe what he says, but I'll follow him and imitate him. I'll love him and revere him. And when I say, "Believe on the Lord Jesus Christ," I mean, not only believing every word He says, but put your foot in every track that Christ ever made toward heaven, and as sure

190

as He is at the right hand of the Father, you will be there, too.

Believe on the Lord Jesus Christ and thou shalt be saved. And, thank God, there is no uncertainty about this: "Believe on the Lord Jesus Christ." It is taking up your cross and following in His footsteps. When He said to Matthew, "Follow me," Matthew followed Him, and I believe to-night Matthew is crowned in eternal glory. Why? Because he followed Christ. There isn't a word in the book about his getting religion, either. But I'll say one thing: There ain't any mystery about this part of it. Whenever an old sinner turns loose all his sins and begins to follow Christ, if he hasn't got religion, what has he got? That has been the question with me. I ain't going to raise any discussion here about what religion is, but I'll go your security with my immortal soul if you'll just quit your meanness and follow along in the footsteps of Jesus Christ. I'll risk my immortality on your safe entrance into the good world up yonder. No mystery in that.

And thou shalt be saved, and thy house. Well, bless you, it looks as if a man gives himself to Christ and Christ gives Himself to the man, that that ought to be enough. But listen—"and thy house."

Thank God, we can go to heaven in families, and I believe that is generally the way we go; and I like to see father and mother gather around a family of children and say, "Children, we're all going to heaven together, or we'll all go to hell together. We're not going to split up the family in eternity." And, brother and sister, if you love your children in this and say, "Children, I'll lead you to heaven or I'll lead you to hell," if you'll talk that way a minute in your mind, you are going to talk right to your children, and you'll be a family in the good world.

191

See the wife taking her husband's arm and walking side by side with him, the two oldest children right behind, and on down to the smallest child, the whole family marching along to the kingdom of everlasting peace! Can any one look on a grander sight than that—a whole family marching into the kingdom of God? Brother, sister, thank God, He will give us our children to go with us.

Now, I haven't time to argue this last point. Let me give you a simple illustration, as told by one of the presiding elders of our conference. He was holding a quarterly conference in Georgia, and one got up and thanked God for a Christian mother and a Christian father, and others got up and thanked God they were raised in the lap of piety, and others thanked God for good parents, and presently a pale, young man, about twenty-two years old—he was then a licentiate Methodist preacher, just licensed—stood up and said:

I'm sorry I can't give the experience of those who have just taken their seats. I wish I could say that I was raised by a pious mother and a good father, but it was to the contrary. Two years ago my father was an atheist, my mother an infidel, and nine brothers and sisters, older than myself, were all infidels and atheists, and I was myself the best I knew how to be. And two years ago I went into an adjoining county to a campmeeting. I happened to go by myself, and went there to have fun, as I usually did. At the first service that night I was standing against one of the posts that held the arbor up, on the outer edge, and all at once every word of the preacher commenced striking fire down in my soul, and I stood transfixed to that post. I felt like I wanted to be away, but yet felt I couldn't leave, and when the preacher ended his sermon and invited up the penitents I went immediately to the altar and knelt down and commenced praying, "God be merciful to me, a sinner," and after a while they dismissed the congregation and all went to the tents, and the preacher came to me and said, "Come out to the tent and we'll pray with you." I looked up at the preacher and told him: "I never knew until an hour ago that there was a God in heaven, and I never expect to leave my knees at this altar till I make Him my friend and He promises me heaven." They sang and prayed with me till one o'clock that night. A little after one, all at once, I felt, indeed and in truth, that I had opened my soul and Christ had come in as my Saviour. And I got up and I slapped my hands together and I said, "I have made friends with God," and I went out of the tent and laid down and went to sleep. Oh, what a peaceful sleep it was, and when I woke up the next morning the bright sun was pouring in through the window of the tent on my face, and I opened my eyes and I thought it was the brightest world I ever looked upon.

After breakfast I got on my horse and started home and this impression came on me: "Your father'll never speak to you again. Your mother'll disown you and your brothers and sisters will all despise you. Now, what have you done?" Oh, how oppressed I was. And just before I got home I turned out in the grove and knelt down and said, "God help me to be faithful. God keep me in this den of lions," and I went on to the house. I took off my better clothes, donned my every-day clothes and went to work. About eight or ten days after I came back from camp-meeting my older brother and I were out cutting rail timber, and about nine o'clock we sat down on a log, and I turned to my brother—I hadn't opened my mouth before to any one—and said: "Brother Tom, do you know I was converted last week down at that camp-meeting?" And such a look as fell on his face, and the great big tears were running down his cheeks, and he said: "Brother Henry, we've all been watching you since you came back from that camp-meeting. Mother says you look and talk like an angel, and sisters say they never saw such a change in a boy in their life, and father says you are the most agreeable one now about the place. Brother Henry, do you reckon God would do for me what He has done for you?" "Why, yes, Brother Tom. A camp-meeting begins to-morrow near here, and I'll go there with you, and I believe God will do for you just what He has done for me."

We went home that night. We never opened our mouths to a single one, and next day brother and I fixed up and put off to that camp-meeting, and the third night after we got there, my brother was soundly converted to God.

"And we came back home and I said, "Brother Tom, let's put our candle on a candlestick, and let it give light to that old dark home. Let's get the Bible down to-night and pray, if mother will let us." And we went on, and after supper, about bedtime, I turned to mother and said: "Mother do you care if Brother Tom and I get down that old dust-covered Bible and read a chapter here to-night and have prayer?" And mother commenced to snub and cry and she said: "Yes, Henry, you come home ten days ago just like an angel, and here comes your brother Tom this evening with the same expression upon his face, and you all can just do anything you please here. God knows in my heart I want just what lights up the countenances of my two boys."

And we got down that old Bible, and I read a chapter and called on Brother Tom to pray, and he got down and knelt on the floor and prayed earnestly for father and mother and children, and I heard mother snubbing over there, and I heard my brother groaning over there, and my sister crying over here, and before we got off our knees my mother was converted and one of my brothers and one of my sisters, and we just kept praying night and morning, until the last member of the family was converted; and there sits my old father, now seventy years old—he was the last one to come in, and now he is clothed and in his right mind and on his way to heaven.

Precious Saviour, fill us so full of thy presence that others seeing our good works may be constrained to glorify thee and our Father which is in heaven.

I wish some of you good men and women out of the church, would be like Dr. Hodges, at Iuka, Miss. He was a river-bottom planter, a man of means, and one of the most cultured men I ever met, about fifty years old. The day I commenced the meeting at Iuka—we held the meeting down in a grove in the Spring Park—I walked down to the spring, and the pastor introduced me to Dr. Hodges and his wife—a magnificent looking gentleman, and his wife, a magnificent woman. When they were gone off, the preacher said, "Dr. Hodges is an atheist and his wife is an infidel."

"Why," said I, "that cultured gentleman an atheist?"

"Yes."

"And that bright woman an infidel?"

"Yes."

But every time I preached—three times a day—I noticed Mrs. Hodges and the doctor sitting in the aisle. I was watching them, and after I had preached three or four days we had an afternoon service, and that woman walked right down the aisle, and I took her hand, and one night I looked in her face and said: "Mrs. Hodges, give your heart to God and be religious. You may be in your grave and in torment before the first day of October. Give your heart to God."

She threw her bright eye up in my face suddenly and said: "What can I do, sir?" I said, "My sister, come up and kneel down there and say 'God, be merciful to me, a sinner,'" and she said: "That can do me no good," and about that time a lady came to me and caught my sleeve and pulled me off; she wanted me to go off to her husband, and I didn't get to talk to this woman any more that night.

Next day, Dr. Hodges was sitting in front of his wife and she farther back. I went out and took his hand in the after service, and said: "Doctor, I'm troubled about you. You are on my heart. I have been praying for you. Won't you give your heart to God?"

He looked up at me with that magnificent, honest face of his, and said: "Mr. Jones, will you please go back to the rostrum there and read the eighth, ninth, and tenth verses of the eleventh chapter of Hebrews?"

Said I, "Yes, sir." I went back and opened the Bible and read, in substance, this: "God called Abraham into a country that he knew not of, and Abraham went, knowing not whither he went. And he sojourned in tabernacles with Isaac and Jacob, the heirs with him of the same promise, and they looked for a city whose builder and maker is God." I read the verses distinctly and sat down, and Dr. Hodges stood up and said: "My fellow countrymen, I have spent my summers for a dozen years here with you all. You are my neighbors and my friends, and I stand up here before you all to confess my sins to God. I have roamed over all the range of science and literature, and nowhere have I found rest for my soul; and to-day my mind goes back to my precious Christian mother and my noble, pious father, and I say, 'Oh, God, take my hand, I know not whither,' and I build a tabernacle here to-day, and I want my precious wife to come in and live with me, and we will look for a city whose maker and builder is God."

Mrs. Hodges rose up and rushed up to the side of her husband and leaned her head on his bosom, with tears just running out of her eyes, and she said, "My husband's God shall be my God, and his people shall be my people, and his peace shall be my peace."

You feel mighty mean to-day and mighty dejected and mighty desolate; but, brother, there's a mighty welcome awaiting you. The angels of God hover over you. . . .

S. J.

10. "COME, YE WEARY AND HEAVY LADEN"

WE INVITE YOUR ATTENTION TO THE TWENTY-SECOND VERSE of the fifty-fifth Psalm:

Cast thy burden upon the Lord and he will sustain thee. He will never suffer the righteous to be moved.

I suppose the greatest curiosity that could be presented to the gaze of this world would be an unburdened human heart—a heart perfectly free from every care and every burden and every anxiety. Four thousand years ago and more a wise man of God said: "Man is born unto trouble as the sparks fly upward."

Just as naturally as the sparks ascend from the burning wood, so naturally is man subjected to trouble. And, after all, the great question of the philosopher is not how many troubles he has, but wisdom to classify troubles, and then to know what to do with them. I grant you that there are a great many imaginary troubles in this world. We are always looking for something we'll never see; we are always going out to meet something that is not coming toward us; we are always expecting something that will never happen. That is human nature. And I reckon the first thing we had better do—because it has much to do with the text and with the discussion—is to classify our troubles. The imaginary we'll call the one class, and the real we'll call the other class.

Imaginary troubles! Home-made trouble we sometimes call this class of troubles. And home-made trouble is like home-made jeans and home-made shoes—they outlast any other sort, and frequently last till we are heartily tired of them. Now, what do I mean by home-made trouble, borrowed trouble, imaginary trouble? I can illustrate it faster than I can present it in any other way.

Here is a good mother, a kind-hearted woman, to say nothing of her strong mind. Her little children come and say: "Mama, let's hitch up old John and drive over to Mrs. Brown's this evening, or up to Mrs. Brown's, or let us go out riding." And kind-hearted mother says: "Well, children, all right." She knows old John is perfectly safe. He is a noted animal. Every man in the community knows old John. And, oh, what a valuable animal he is, because of being so trustworthy, so gentle. Some of the little children can go down into the lot and climb up his legs, he is so humble, and they can hitch him up to a sleigh or buggy or anything, and, really, when the children come around him on the lot and grass and play around him, he puts a foot down and seems to shake it to see whether any of the little fellows' fingers or feet are under his hoofs. Old John has learned to love the children, and he seems to think as much of them as mother does.

And this is the horse they hitch up. And nothing is thought until the clock strikes four—that is the hour they promised to be back—and the clock strikes four, and mother looks up and says: "The children haven't come back, and they promised to be back at four o'clock. They have never deceived me before in their life. I am satisfied something has happened."

Now, you see she will start her trouble-machine at that point—and an old trouble-machine is like one of those old looms. Did you ever see an old woman at her loom? I can just remember having seen an old woman, a good woman sitting, with both feet working the pedal and both hands throwing the broach, or the shuttle, and the spool of broach in her mouth—hands and feet and mouth all going just as hard as she can run them. And I have seen these trouble-machines start hand, heart, soul, foot, spirit, body, everything at work together, conjuring up trouble.

And this good wife thinks, "Well, now, I know something has happened." The minute finger points fifteen minutes overtime. "I know something has happened. And the fact of the business is, I recollect now, I had a presentiment the other day that that horse was going to run away and kill every child I had. The Lord knows I am not fit for a mother. I am not worthy to have any children. And, in addition to that, I recollect now, the last time I drove old John he took a fearful fright, and I said right then I never would let those children ride that horse again. The Lord knows, I am the most careless creature, and I deserve nothing better than that every child I have in the world should be dead on the roadside right now, and I am satisfied they are for a judgment on me."

Well, about this time the old gentleman walks in, and he sees the situation. "Wife, what in the world is the matter?"

"Well," she says, "I gave the children permission to drive old John off this afternoon, and they promised to be back at four o'clock, and it's past four o'clock, and they haven't come, and they promised me they would; and you know, husband, they never told me a story in their life." "Why, wife," says the husband, "they tell them here every day."

Anything to run your trouble mill!

"Well," she says, "I had a presentiment about those children being killed by that horse." "Why, wife, you're always having something. Hush! those children will be here directly." And she says: "Yes, and I never told you about that horse getting so frightened with me the other day, and I know those children are killed, and I want you to go right off and bring them back, dead or alive, and do it quick. I'll be crazy in a minute." "Wife, I ain't going off to bother about those children. They'll be here directly." "Well," she says, "if you don't go, I'll go myself."

And well he knows what that means. And he starts right off, and about the time he gets to the front gate, here comes old John jogging up in his old camp-meeting trot, and stops right in front of the gate, and the children light out with a laugh of merriment, and mother looks on the picture and goes back in her room and sits down and buries her face in her hands and says, "What a goose I have been."

And I say so, too. That is exactly my judgment. And of all the geese the world ever saw, the featherless goose is the most ridiculous.

I saw her at church one day. She didn't seem to hear one word I said. She was looking out the window, she was looking out the door, and as soon as I pronounced the benediction she hurried to her buggy and drove off at breakneck speed, and I learned afterward that she left a little fire at home in the old fireplace, and she thought the house was afire and she was looking out every moment to see the flames and the smoke, and when the service was dismissed she hurried off home, expecting at every turn of the wheels to see the flames and smoke burst out, and directly she drove up to the house and unlocked the door and went in, and there was a dead pile of ashes in her fireplace, and she looked at it and said: "Law, me, what a goose I have been!"

Women are not the only creatures in this world. I am sorry they do borrow trouble. But I am sorry to say they are not the only ones. Oh, me, how we men borrow trouble! And all the trouble we have, brother!

There's many a man in this house that has rolled and tumbled in his bed over some problem that he ought to have gone to sleep over at nine o'clock and woke up fresh the next morning, and started out to work out his problem. Did you know that a bed was made to sleep in, and that God sent night in this world so we could sleep and rest for the next day's battles? And, oh, how wickedly foolish a man is who tries to work out his problems at night instead of sleeping. And he says: "Well, the fact of the matter is, David said, 'I have been young, and now am old, and I have never seen the righteous forsaken or his seed begging bread.' But this something don't happen; I'll see it this time. I can say that much. I just tell you what, starvation is right at the door. I have made buckle and tongue meet up to this time, but they'll never meet any more." And there he worries!

A good deal like the old woman that prayed God for twenty years to give her grace to die in the poorhouse. She had an elegant mansion and that was the burden of her prayers for twenty years: "Good Lord, give me grace to die in the poorhouse," and at last she died in an elegant mansion worth $30,000. The Lord will never let a person die in a poorhouse when he is going to die rich. You need not go to Him about these things. And I speak about this to you all, that we each may classify his trouble.

If a man is young and strong and vigorous, what does

he need to borrow trouble about the bread and meat question? As God is my judge, I was born poor and raised poor, and I never worried about a meal in my life up to this hour —I never did. I never want to. I never want to take any more trouble to bed with me than I can kick off in one lick, and off altogether.

The devil has got a great big joke on a Christian when he can keep him awake half the night, and I imagine when the devil bids some Christians good-by he will turn around and say: "He has gone to glory, but I had enough fun out of him before he left, and you can take him along." I am not going to be joked that way. I am not going to be kicked around that way. I have the promise of God's word that if I trust Him and do good I shall overwhelm the land and be fed, and as long as the lambs and the orphans are fed, I know God will take care of the man who trusts Him. And it is right enough to be true.

And I have often thought of the sound philosophy of the man I heard of once. In an upper room a man was walking till the clock struck twelve, and struck one, and struck two, and the fellow down in the room below wanted to go to sleep, and he could not go to sleep for that man's walking. Finally, he got up and dressed himself, and went upstairs and knocked at the door, and the man in the room opened the door, and said: "Friend, what in the world is the matter with you? I cannot go to sleep, with you walking the floor." "Why," said the walker, "I owe $10,000 and it is due to-morrow, and I have done my best, and I cannot pay it." "Do you say you have done your best and you cannot pay it?" "Yes." "Why, my friend, if you have done your best, go to bed and go to rest and let the other fellow do the walking; he is the fellow that has got to do the walking now." I will worry over anything, but let the other fellow do the walking after nine o'clock. I will go to sleep and let the other fellow do the walking.

Trouble! Borrowed trouble, home-made trouble, and all that sort of thing. As I have said, I have been worried. I might have troubled a great deal, I think. Among the hardest months of my ministry, depending on God and doing my duty, I have seen my home when the last bite we had in the world was on the table, and I knew it, and I told wife that evening, and I went out to cut stove wood to get supper, and there was not a thing in the closet, there was not a thing in the pantry, and she said, "I tell you, it is all out." "Well," said I, "I have done my best, and I have preached and worked and prayed, and tried to do my whole duty, and," said I, "wife, we'll just stick it out right here, and if we starve to death we'll make out like we died of typhoid fever." Well, sir, that night, before supper, a wagon drove into my yard, and when it unloaded its good things into my house I had more to eat at one time than I ever had before or have had since.

No trouble about those things. Trust God and do right, and don't bother about anything you cannot help. In daytime put in your best licks, and at night sleep soundly, like you had pillowed your head on the bosom of the God who made you.

Well, the reason I talk this way is not to tickle your humor at all—we have got over beyond that in this meeting—but to show you this much, you must contradistinguish, you must separate, you must classify.

Now, that good sister need not have dropped down on her knees and asked the Lord to head old John, and stop old John. The Lord ain't going to head old John, when he ain't running away. And you need not ask the Lord to put out the fire in your house when it is not on fire. He is too busy to do that. And you need not ask the Lord to keep you from starving, when the Lord is in heaven and knows you won't starve. Let us classify these things.

There is but one remedy for borrowed trouble, there is but one remedy for home-made trouble, there is but one remedy for heart trouble, and that is good, old, hard, common sense, and bring your hard common sense to bear on these things and sweep them out of your way, just as you would with cobwebs.

But let us come to the real troubles—and these are the hardest. They have shape and form and being.

There are real troubles in life that touch us all along the line. There are burdens that I cannot bear, and that you cannot bear. There are burdens to-day pressing on millions of hearts in this world—burdens that an angel would shudder at if he had to carry them an hour. Oh, how many burdens press on the hearts of mothers and fathers and children all over this world!

And I will say another thing: There is a point beyond which you cannot go with your load. I have said it a thousand times; and said it because I felt it. I believe if it was not for the cross of Jesus Christ the great heart of this world would break. We cannot carry the burdens.

Brethren, what are my real burdens and what are your real burdens? There are the burdens of anxiety that press sorely on many a heart.

My Brother Blackwell, the pastor of the Cumberland Presbyterian church, stood in St. John's this morning and told us how his godly father in the pulpit stood with his eye fixed on him and preached earnestly, and in the exhortation said: "Come to-night," and he was watching his godless boy, and as the father looked at him and said "Come to-night," the pressure on his heart was so great that he trembled a moment and then fell prostrate in the pulpit and died. Oh, how that boy saw the pressure on his father's heart! The father carried it until he threw it down in death. And, thank God, he never carried it beyond death.

I visited the Insane Asylum of Georgia when I was preaching at Milledgeville. I went through the wards with the keeper, and as we walked through, I saw the distorted face of a once pure, sweet mother. As we passed by, the doctor said: "There is the wife of Mr. So-and-so. There is the mother of a family of children." And I looked back and thought "Mother, mother, what tore you away from your home? Mother, what robbed you of the care of your children? What took you from the side of your husband? What shut you up in this doleful place? Mother, what did it?" And her very face spoke the answer back: "Trouble did this; trouble did this."

You go yonder to that hotel to-morrow morning, any morning, some morning, and there is a poor suicide. The pistol is lying at his side. The derringer ball entered his temple. He is covered with his own blood. And as I look at the poor corpse, baptized in its own blood, I say: "Oh, man, man, what did this? What did this?" And he speaks back in unmistakable language: "Trouble did this. I got more than I could carry."

Trouble! This incident I read some time ago of a mother! She was sitting in company with a dozen other ladies in a parlor, and the conversation turned on trouble. One related her trouble, and another hers, and another hers, until, at last, every one had spoken except a pale, sad-faced lady, and they turned to her and said: "You have not told us your trouble."

Oh [she said], ladies, I have been listening to your troubles, but I have thought your troubles are merely bubbles on life's current. They are

> "Like the snowflake on the river,
> A moment white, then melts forever."

But I have had trouble. I was raised in affluence, and never knew a want. My husband was also wealthy, and we united our fortunes, and settled on our beautiful plantation on the banks of the Savannah river. And we lived there happily and peacefully for a number of years, and God had blessed us with five sweet children. One night I woke up. My hand dropped out of the side of the bed, and it touched a current of water in my room. I waked my husband up immediately, and the water was eighteen inches deep. He rushed for the children and saw they were all safe, and he got me and the children out of the house onto a little knoll right by. We stood there only a moment, and we saw the water coming higher and higher [it was one of those waterspouts that caused this unheard of rapid rise in the river] and husband stood there a moment and said: "Wife, I will take you and the babes to the hillside where you will be safe."

He carried me and my children to the hillside, and as he came back through the valley between two of those mounds, one of those fearful spouts came sweeping down and carried him and swept him out, and I have never seen his face since. But that was not trouble. I stood there under the pale light of the moon and saw the turbid waters rise to my child next to the baby, and the troubled waters rose a moment and swept him out of sight, and I have never seen him since. I stood there until the waters rose above the head of the next and carried him out of my sight. I stood there until the waters stood up to the very neck and mouth of my oldest child. I stood there a moment, and the little child struggled and went out of sight, and I have never seen my husband or one of those children since. But that was not trouble. I thought it was. That left me with the precious little babe in my arms—all I had left. I trained and nurtured that child until he was seventeen years old, and then, a pure, good boy, I sent him off to college.

There is the doom of thousands of boys: "I sent him off to college. I sent him off to college."

Would anybody think from that remark, and the repeating of that remark, that I do believe in colleges and education? Yes, sir, I believe in them as much as any man in this house, but I have said, and I repeat it, I'd rather see my boy in heaven learning his A B C's than to have him sit down in hell and read Greek forever. All unsanctified knowledge is degrading!

Just let us take that thought—and that is my sentiment exactly on that line. I am willing to be taken for an ignoramus, but I am never willing to be taken for a rascal. Do you understand that? I can afford to be called a fool, but God save me from anything that will make anybody think I am a rascal.

I was tickled with a kind, clever boy in this city. He was sitting down and talking to me kindly, and said he: "Mr. Jones, how far did you go in your education? Did you go far?" "Well, sir," I said, "I got so I could lay all round Latin and just handle Greek right along. Why?" "Well," he said, "most of them are talking about your appearing to be very ignorant and you don't know much, and I've been out several times and I think they're mistaken."

I say you can afford to be taken for a poor, ignorant fellow, but God keep you and me from being anything that will put us in the other list. I reckon we'll have little else to do in heaven but learn forever. If I can keep from sin down here, then God will help me in heaven to learn His lessons there.

Now to go back to the story I was telling. The woman said:

I sent my boy off to college. When he came back home he was dissipated, wicked, unruly, godless, in all his ways. Oh, how wicked he was. I did my best and lavished every kindness and all my wealth on that boy, and he went from bad to worse and from bad to worse, until at last, at last, I received a newspaper yesterday giving an account of my boy's being hung in a distant State, and he died a felon's death, on a felon's gallows, and has gone to a felon's hell. Oh, here's trouble! Here's trouble!

Oh, how many hearts in the house carry weights that an angel would shudder at if he had them to carry.

Brother Brookes—I am very sorry to be called on to interrupt our brother again, but some one at the door wants to see Dr. Scott immediately. Probably it is a case of sickness, and as such ought to be attended to. I'm sorry we have to make this announcement.

Brother Jones, do you know the necessity for the doctor? Do you know what makes it necessary for such calls as that? Sometimes there are thousands of people that would unload every burden of their souls and throw them away forever. Do you know what pain in the soul is? Pain in the soul is to the soul just what physical pain is to the body. Do you know what pain is to the body? I wake up this morning and this lung! Oh, it pains me! What is pain? It is the voice of the physical nature crying out, "Send for the doctor! Something is wrong! Something wrong! Hurry! No time to lose! Go to the church and have the announcement made!" When there is something wrong the pain speaks out. And every trouble, every pang of your soul, tells you, "Something is wrong. Send for the Great Physician." And the Great Physician now is near, the sympathizing Jesus. And just what pain is to my body, just so trouble is to my soul. "Something wrong! Send for the Great Physician." Something may be wrong with the child; then tell Him about it. Something may be wrong with the house; tell your Great Physician about it. Oh, friends hear me. This trouble! trouble! trouble! It is the warning voice of God to my soul, telling me, "Something wrong! Send for the Great Physician."

Trouble! There are the troubles and there are the burdens of grief, the burdens of anxiety, burdens of a thousand kind that press on us. The burden of guilt—oh, how it presses on poor human nature! Here's a poor sinner, sick, laden, heavy laden! Oh, look at him as he presents his case before the throne, undone, wretched, borne down with the pressure of guilt enough to crush a world, and there he is, with his burden of guilt. He comes to God with it. He comes to Christ with his burden, and the great Burden-bearer takes his burden off him and tells him to go in peace.

Oh, the burden of guilt! I have felt it a thousand times. I have felt down in the depths of my soul that I am the most guilty wretch in all the universe. I have knelt in sight of the cross, and, oh, how gloriously and grandly Christ would lift that burden from my soul!

Bunyan represents his pilgrim as reaching the Wicket Gate and passing up to the cross, and the burden rolled off him and he stands upright before God. And no man can ever stand upright before God until his burden rolls off him.

Oh, how it presses us down! I have hung my head many a time when there was not a man within a mile of me who could have told what I was hanging it about. Oh, conscious guilt! "The guilty flee when no man pursueth."

The burden of guilt! Guilty before God! Guilty before man! Oh, the guilt I carry in my bosom! How many can say that? The burden of my guilt!

Then there's the burden of grief. Every black veil in

this congregation carries on its very texture a history. Oh, the bereavements, and the burden of bereavements!

Death came to my humble cottage home when I was not a Christian. It was the darkest hour in my life's history. God blessed wife and me with a sweet little cherub. She was just nineteen months old. She was so playful and joyous and happy. Wife took the baby and ran down on a visit to my sister in another State. The day they were to come home I had gone to town and bought some nice little presents for that sweet little child. I thought, "This evening I'll take her in my arms and I'll see her eyes dance and her little pink fingers catch at the nice things, and I shall see her little heart made glad." Wicked like I was, the highest aspiration of my heart was to make my child happy and glad. I walked down town after dinner and here came one of those fearful telegrams: "Little Beulah is very ill. Come immediately."

I started with a weight that almost crushed me, and on my way there I dozed off into a disquieted sleep two or three times, and each time dreamed that I had that sweet, little, playful thing in my arms, and I would wake up and say, "I know she's better."

I had to go part of the way in a buggy, and when I drove up to the front gate my wife came to the door. I shall never forget how she looked. My heart sank. I went into the parlor, and there was something so unusual to be seen in a parlor. I walked in with my wife clinging to my arm, and I turned back the beautiful white cloth, and there was my sweet child looking like a little angel chiseled out of marble. I put my hand on her face, and it was so cold; I went into the other room and just fell down and cried like a child. Oh, how cheerless! How dark! How dark! How dark! Oh, how these burdens press on these poor hearts of ours! The burden of grief!

But I can say this much to you: God has one of my children. I committed it to Him forever, and I say this much: My other sweet children have a much better father than they ever would have had if they had not a sweet little sister in heaven. I am a better father to my children than I ever would have been if it had not been for the precious one that has gone, and I'm going to try to train—I'm going to try to venture—I'm going to try to keep my children in the path that they may meet that sweet one up yonder.

Oh, the burden of grief! Where is the heart in this house that has never been pressed down in its pilgrimage to the grave? This is a world of burdens. And then there is the burden of anxiety. I have seen wives who were literally crushed with burdens of anxiety.

At Iuka, Miss., I recollect a wife came to the altar, and knelt down, and prayed, and prayed, and, by and by, when the others had walked away, I said to her: "Now, can't you trust it all to God?" She said, "I tell you, Mr. Jones, I have been praying for my husband for weeks and months and years, and I'm going to stay right here until my husband gives his heart to God."

I had met her husband, the coldest-blooded infidel I ever looked in the face in my life. "Well," said I, "sister, if I were you I would talk and pray with my husband at home." "No," she said, "I have done my best, and right here I'm going to stay on my knees until my husband gives his heart to God."

I walked back in the congregation, went up to that man, and gave him my hand. Said I: "Sir, there are no weapons that were ever manufactured in the United States, loaded

213

and cocked in my face ready to fire at me, that could keep me from going to my wife if she had such a burden on her heart as your wife has. Go up there and kneel down and give your heart to God." "Oh," he said, "Mr. Jones, I am not concerned about religion. I don't want to be a hypocrite." Said I: "My friend, how can you break your wife's heart?"

I went back to her and said, "Your husband won't come."

"Well," she said, "he has not come; but I'll never get off my knees until my husband gives his heart to God."

The first thing I knew he was there, right by her. And when the first prayer was over with, he got up, and then tried to get her off her knees. She looked at him and said: "Have you surrendered your heart to God, sir?"

"No," he said.

"Well, I'll never get off from here until you do."

We knelt and prayed again, and soon that husband got up, and said: "Wife, get up now."

She said: "Have you surrendered to God, sir, and will you seek Him until you find him?"

He looked down at her and said: "Yes."

"Well," she said, "husband, you never deceived me in my life. You never told me a falsehood in my life, and I take you at your word, sir, and I believe God Almighty will do now just what I have been asking him to do."

And it looked like that wife would have died there on her knees. Oh, the pressure! the pressure! the pressure! I have carried such burdens for those I loved. Oh, brother, you are burdened with these things that press sorely on you, sorely on you!

Well, now, the great question is another matter. We won't discuss the burdens any longer. There are thousands

214

that press on our heart. Now, the part of a philosopher is this, to know what to do with our burdens.

What will we do with them? What can I do? It is not wise to sit down and count them to see how many I have, or how crushing they are, or to think about other people's burdens. But what will I do with them? The answer comes thus: "Cast thy burden upon the Lord, and he will sustain thee. He will never suffer the righteous to be moved."

That is why you have your burdens. I wouldn't refuse to take one, but I'll use them wisely if they come on me. Here, you see, is a Newfoundland dog, swimming out yonder in that lake at will. His master stands on the bank and calls him, but he won't come. He beckons and the dog won't come. He rebukes, and the dog won't come. And then the master stoops and picks up a little stick and pitches it into the lake near the dog, and the dog swims to it and catches it in his mouth, and swims to his master and puts it down at his feet. That was the only way his master could get him to come.

Many a time, brother, sister, we have wandered off on the sea of sin and death, away from God, and He calls us, and we won't come; and He beckons us, and we won't come; and He rebukes, and we won't come. And then God pitches a crushing burden on our hearts, and with that burden He says: "Now, bring it back and lay it down at my feet. I'll hear your cause and heal all your wounds."

Blessed be God! Every burden of the life is to bring me back to God. It is a message from God to bring it to Him: "Bring it to me."

Oh, many are the hearts in this house that are overloaded! You see that little frail vessel yonder as she is pitching and tossing on the rolling ocean, and she's overloaded. Now and again, the waves sweep over her bulwarks and she is about to go down under her fearful weight, and the captain says to the crew: "We must all go down to the bottom, everything."

And about that time the *Great Eastern*, the grandest vessel that ever swam the Atlantic Ocean, came plowing along right up beside the little frail vessel, and the captain of the *Geat Eastern* walks up to the outer edge of her bulwark and looks down at the frail little vessel and crew, and he says: "You're overloaded! Cast your cargo on me. I can carry it for you on this grand old ship so you can make port in safety." And the crew go to work with block and tackle, and they lift out their cargo until they have lightened their ship so it can go on its way rejoicing, and it doesn't sink the *Great Eastern* the hundredth part of an inch. She scarcely knows that she has taken on any more burden.

And here we are, out on the sea of sin and death, our frail little human vessel overloaded, and we are about to go down with everything, and right about this time the grand old ship of Zion plows its way along right up by our side and its good captain steps over to the bulwark and looks down at the frail, sinking ship, and says: "Cast your burden on me. I'll carry it for you. It won't sink me the hundredth part of an inch, and in that way you can make port in safety." And we cast our burden on him, and then we go along and say: "Now, thank God,

> 'Not a wave of trouble rolls
> Across my peaceful breast.'

I have found my heavenly home. The burden has been taken off me." And the little boat strikes a beeline for the shore of everlasting deliverance.

Brethren, I want to say this: Whenever you get in

trouble, you can go to Christ, and trust in Christ. I have found that out.

Blessed Jesus! When His disciples were smoothly sailing on the lake, He went there in earnest prayer, not noticing anything, but one of those fearful little squalls came down on the lake and pitched the disciples and their little ship hither and thither, and was about to engulf them. But Jesus looked down on that little lake, and said: "My disciples are in danger!" and He rushed down the mountain side and stood on the bank of the little lake and saw them as they were pitching and tossing, and He looked around, and there was no boat there for Him to ride out to them. He looked again, said: "My disciples are in danger and trouble, and I'm going to them, boat or no boat." Down He moved, right to the water, and ran out and stopped the boat, and immediately it came to shore.

I tell you, brother, you are not far from land—whenever Christ gets on board you are not far from the shore of heaven. "Cast your burden on the Lord and he shall sustain thee. He will never suffer the righteous to be moved."

Brother! Brother! Young man! Father! Husband! Hear me a minute now. Let's you and I help unload mother's heart! Let's you and I help unload wife's heart! Let's you and I help unload our children's hearts.

Oh, me! The most touching incident in my ministry is when some little girl, twelve years old, comes up and says: "Mr. Jones, please, sir, pray for papa. He is so wicked, and he won't come to church." And then comes up another little girl, and says: "Mr. Jones, the Lord has blessed me, but I am so anxious about papa."

Oh, brother! brother! Let's you and I, in God, unload wife's heart! My wife carried me like a million-pound weight on her heart for months and months and months.

I owed my wife a debt I never could pay until I paid it at the cross, and my wife unloaded this burden at the cross, and since that time, oh, how glorious and joyous her life has been in that respect!

Brother, let's you and I meet wife at the cross! Let's you and I, young man, meet precious, good mother at the cross! Oh, boys, look at mama's gray hairs! Look at those wrinkles in mother's face! And, say, boys, did you ever plow one of those wrinkles there? Did you ever cause one of those hairs to turn gray?"

I met on the train, some time ago, a drummer. Said he: "Mr. Jones, I was very much touched the other day. I got a letter from my mother. It was a sweet, good letter, but," he said, "it wasn't mother's words that troubled me so. It was not how she wrote. It was not what she said. It was the tremulous hand on the paper." He said, "Mother has nearly done writing to her boy. And, Mr. Jones, that letter has touched me, and before God I want to be a joy to my mother the balance of her life."

Boys, let's think about precious mother! Husbands, let's think about wife! Neighbor, let's think about neighbor! Let's go to work to-night and unload every burden that we have ever put on anybody's heart! Won't you?

I tell you how I think about it. If in innocence I have put a care or burden on anybody's heart I would walk till daylight came to take that burden off his heart. If my precious wife has a burden on her heart on my account, or of one of my children, I would walk till daylight and lift with all my power to get that burden off. The fact of the business is, mother has got as much as she can carry, without us troubling her. Poor wife has all she can carry, without us putting on any more. Oh, brother, let's you and I never wring another tear from mother's eye or another sigh from wife's lips!

David knew what he was talking about. Listen:

Give ear to my prayer, O God, and hide not thyself from my supplication. Attend unto me and hear me: I mourn in my complaint and make a noise. Because of the voice of the enemy, because of the oppression of the wicked. My heart is sore pained within me, and the terrors of death are fallen upon me. And I said: Oh, that I had wings like a dove! for then would I fly away and be at rest. Lo, then would I wander afar off and remain in the wilderness.

Brother, I have felt that way many a time—"Oh, that I had wings like a dove." I have felt, "Well, I am just weighted down; all the pressure of my ministry on me, the care of my family and ten thousand burdens that mothers and wives have put upon my heart," and I have almost literally stood in many a wife's tracks with burdens on my soul for this one and for that one and for the other one, and I have carried these burdens until I have felt in my heart —"Oh, that I had wings like a dove," that I might fly away to some peaceful mountain and have one week's rest, that I might forget that I had a wife and children, forget that I was called to preach, forget everything in the universe and just have one week's happy rest. I have felt like I could come back to this world a new man, that I would be new all over. "Oh, that I had wings like a dove, that I might fly away and be at rest."

I have carried burdens. I have carried them, but, blessed be God, I have learned this blessed text now: "Cast your burdens on the Lord, and he will sustain you."

Just think about that! Is there any trouble anywhere? Then take it all to Jesus in prayer. Just take your burdens

219

and lay them down at His feet. That is all we can do with them. And I have seen thousands of souls come up and throw their burdens down at the foot of the cross and go away singing:

> Now not a wave of trouble rolls
> Across my peaceful breast.

Let us put our burdens at Christ's feet! Let us throw them all down there, whether of sin or guilt or anxiety or grief. Let us cast them all at His feet, and say: "Blessed Christ! there they are. I can carry them no farther."

Thank God! It won't be much longer till "the wicked cease from troubling, and the weary are at rest."

I have thought—tired and worn out, I have thought—of that world of rest. I have thought of that world where there is no pain or trouble; where there shall be no more tears. "For God shall wipe away all tears from their eyes."

I have thought about that expression very much like this:

I am sitting here in the family room with mother, and here comes little six-year-old Annie crying like her little heart would break, the tears just raining from her little face. And the mother says: "What is it, darling? Don't cry." But Annie says: "Mama, I can't help it." And while the tears are raining down, mama takes the little girl and says: "There's a sweet darling; don't cry."

But she says: "Mama, I can't help it." And she is throwing tears from one and the other, and mother reaches out her gentle hand and catches her little girl's arms and pulls her up against her knees, and puts her gentle hand over this eye and then over that eye, and the tears are gone, and they don't appear any more.

And then I have thought, as we pass into the gates of

everlasting deliverance, the blessed Christ will run His gentle fingers over these eyes that have been drowned with tears a thousand times, and my tears will be gone forever. That's God! No tears there! No sadness there! No sickness there! No pain there, forever!

Oh, brother, let us start to that good world now.

A good many people are going to be good when they get to heaven. Well, old fellow, you'd better be good down here or you won't get in.

S. J.

11. CHRISTIAN FAITH AND CHRISTIAN LIFE

WE INVITE YOUR ATTENTION TO THE 17th VERSE OF THE 7th chapter of the Gospel of St. John:

If any man will do his will, he shall know of the doctrine, whether it be of God, or whether I speak of myself.

We will read three of the preceding verses:

Now about the midst of the feast Jesus went up into the temple, and taught. And the Jews marveled, saying, How knoweth this man letters, having never learned? Jesus answered them, and said, My doctrine is not mine, but his that sent me.

At the time Jesus uttered these words He was surrounded by the sharp, calculating Sadducees and the shrewd, cunning Pharisees, and the probing, dissecting minds of the lawyers of His day. They were doubting; they were hating; they were despising; they were wondering. It is natural for man to doubt; it is very common for man to despise; and very frequently we are made to wonder at some things. It is as natural for a man to doubt as it is for him to live a sinner, and I suppose some of you find that very natural! A great many think, "Well, I am a sinner, because I am an infidel," but you are an infidel because you are a sinner. You have got the thing reversed. A man does not sin because he doubts; he doubts because he sins.

I believe the quickest, clearest, grandest conversion God had under His own immediate ministry was the case of Nathaniel. When Nathaniel came up into the presence of Christ, Christ dropped his finger on him and said: "Behold an Israelite indeed, in whom there is no guile."

And the doors of Nathaniel's heart flew wide open and he said "My Lord and my God." The quickest, clearest, grandest conversion of Jesus' ministry was the case of Nathaniel. He was without guile, and a heart without guile always opens itself when Christ is near.

We sin, and doubt because we sin. I said once before you never had a doubt in your life but that if you would take hold of it and pull it up by the roots you would find there was a seed at the bottom of the taproot, and the name of that seed is Sin. And if you will quit sinning, you will quit doubting just as naturally as possible.

Now, these scribes and Pharisees and lawyers stood around Christ, all probing, all despising, all wondering and all hypocrites. The Bible has a good deal to say about hypocrisy and about hypocrites, but nine-tenths of all the hypocrites I ever saw were out of the church. They do not belong to the church at all. When a man out there says he is as good as anybody, if he could get anybody to believe him he would be a first-class hypocrite, but his unreliability saves him from the charge of hypocrisy. Nobody believes him and therefore he passes for what he is worth. If that man out there could create the impression that he had done as much good as anybody he would be a first-class hypocrite. His failure to make the impression saves him from the charge of being a hypocrite.

Do you know what a hypocrite is? A hypocrite is a man

that don't do right, but wants to make people believe he is doing right. It takes all these elements to make a hypocrite. Now, how many hypocrites do you know in the churches of this town that do not do right, who want to make people believe they do right, and who don't want to do right? How many hypocrites have you in the churches of this town, according to that rule? And it is not so much whom you look at as it is what sort of a fellow is looking at you. There is a good deal in that. A dozen stood round looking at Christ, and Christ dropped His finger on them and said, "Whom say you—you, you and you—that I am?" And they said, "You are an impostor, and you are a blasphemer, and you are the son of—a harlot." And Jesus looked over to Peter, who was standing there, and said, "Peter, whom say ye I am?" I wish I could have seen Peter about that time. Just lifting his face up, he said: "Thou art the Christ, the Son of the living God." Peter was a man just like the rest of them, but Peter had got into a secret they did not know much about.

We say a man doubts only as he sins, and that he will doubt as long as he is a sinner. But if you want to believe and believe with all your heart, empty your heart of guile, empty your heart of all sin, strip yourself of all this, and then you take in God for all He can do for a soul.

You have heard Christian people say, "Oh, I have so many doubts." Well, it is no credit to them. I will say that, and if I were they I would keep it to myself. You just size yourself up as a great big sinner if you have great big doubts. One is the result of the other.

"My Lord and my God" is the language of the man who saw Christ for the first time, and he took Christ into his soul the first time he had an opportunity. There is something very practical on the human side of salvation, whatever you may say about the mysteries on the other side, and I have noticed that the practical discharge of the duties God imposes on us makes a great many mysteries very plain to us. I have found that out.

Now, I grant you that in all the ages of the world the great discoverers of this world have met with doubts and opposition, and frequently with doom. You may take Galileo, who asserted the discovery of Copernicus, that this world rotates on its axis. He was arraigned, tried, and convicted as the greatest heretic this world ever saw. And they laughed his theory to scorn and made him retract it, and yet when he walked out from that august body he turned and said: "And yet the world rolls on." And to-day any little schoolboy in this town will tell you that the world rotates on its axis and rolls round the sun in its yearly revolution. I believe every being in the universe has accepted the theory that the world moves round the sun, except Jasper, the preacher, at Richmond. I heard the other day he was dead. I would hate to have such a case to funeralize. I would preach him to heaven, though, on the ground of downright ignorance, for I think there are a good many going there on that platform. All opposition to this grand discoverer has died away long ago. The world has accepted his theory and praises its author for it to-day.

When Harvey discovered that the blood circulated from the heart to the extremities and back again to the heart, he was arraigned by the world. They admitted that the earth rotated on its axis, but they would not admit that the blood circulated. They tried Harvey and convicted him as the greatest heretic this world ever saw. Yet now we honor him as one of earth's greatest discoverers, and to-day, when the physician walks into your sick room and lays his finger on your pulse, he determines the nature of the disease by the accelerated action of the pulse, which is the indicator of the arterial circulation. No one doubts now that the blood circulates.

When Watt discovered that steam—a bland vapor—had a power almost omnipotent, the world laughed him to scorn, and arraigned him, tried him, and convicted him as the greatest heretic the world ever saw. And when Stephenson constructed his engine, that infidel world stood and looked on, ready to laugh him to scorn; but when he pulled back the throttle and the engine moved off before the gaze of an infidel world with an astonishing power and velocity, the world hung its head. "We give up." Can anybody doubt the power of steam who sees these iron horses moving over this country a mile a minute, pulling their freighted tons over it? All opposition to this grand discoverer has died out with the past.

When Morse discovered that a man might chain electricity to a wire, and that one man might sit in one city and talk to a person in another city in private conversation, the world pricked up its ears and said, "We have a sure-enough humbug now, and we will condemn him without trial. It's the most astounding humbug the world ever saw; there is no truth in it." Who doubts now that I can go into a telegraph office in this town and talk for an hour to a friend in Liverpool, England? And I say of these grand discoverers who have proclaimed these discoveries to the world, that in this day the world builds monuments to them and honors them!

But the grandest discoverer in this world's history was He who 1,800 years ago discovered the balm of Gilead and poured His own precious blood out to redeem this world. That precious blood has been washing its millions for 1,800 years, and yet, to-day, after all the triumphs of the cross and the cleansing power of the blood, there is as much opposition from science to-day to the Christ crucified as there ever was in any age of the world. I reckon we would have been fighting Galileo to-day if he had abused dram-drinking, cursing, and making money. I expect we would have been fighting Harvey on the same line. I expect we will fight anything that proposes to abridge our privileges to go to hell. Oh, why is it that we accept everything from everybody that is proven true, and yet when the blood-washed throng in heaven, and the best of earth stand up and testify to Jesus' power to save, there are those who have doubts and misgivings about His power to save a soul to God?

Thank God, 1,800 years ago, before I ever saw the light of this world, that precious blood was shed to redeem me, and thank God, 1,800 years after it was poured out my poor heart was washed in the blood Jesus Christ had poured out to save sinners. Now, brother, I say this, and I talk with the Bible open before me, and with intelligent men and women before me. Listen. The science of Christ crucified, the religion of Christianity, may be tested just like anything else. A great many say it is a sentiment for old women and children. I recollect in the town where I lived that there was a poor fellow whom they called half-witted. All the sense he had in the world was religious sense, and all the sense he had was good sense—pious sense. And they used to dub him a crank and say he was crazy. They said he was crazy on the subject of religion, and I told the people they would all feel like there had been an eternal practical joke played on them, when they walked up to the bar of God for judgment, to find that poor Gus, whom they had called crazy, was the only sensible man in the town. Let me say to those who speak of the religion of

Jesus Christ as the plaything of an idiot, or as a sentiment for a poor old woman in her dotage to hug to her heart, that there is something in it to engage the grandest minds and keep busy the biggest hearts this world ever saw. Let us stop to think before we deride the religion that has blood-washed the world already and that proposes to save me and my child from the sins that beset us and make us meet and fit for the Master's house in heaven.

Now we stop for a moment. The science of mathematics, for instance, is a true science that has been demonstrated to be true. A man tells a class: "True it is that the science is true." I will say: "Demonstrate it to me." He says: "Twice two are four."

I say, "Hush, that is child's talk. Now demonstrate to me that mathematics is a true science."

And he says, "Six times six are thirty-six."

I say, "I do not want any foolishness. I want a grand demonstration that the science of mathematics is a true science."

He says: "You are a sensible man, and I will take you over here to these Alps," those grand mountains piled up there between France and Switzerland. Those two Governments want to tunnel that mountain, and they want to begin on opposite sides of the mountain and meet each other in the middle of the mountain. Millions are involved in the undertaking, and the science of mathematics starts up and says: "I will guide you through that old dark mountain and bring you together in the heart of it." "But," say these Governments, "if you fail to do it we have lost millions." The engineers say they will not fail, and they bring their instruments to bear on that old mountain and mark out the lines.

They work there for weeks and months and years, and

229

thousands are spent, and people wonder how this is going to come out. One day the workmen on France's side sat down to dinner. The workmen on Switzerland's side rose from their midday meal and commenced work first. The French workmen suddenly heard the rumblings of the pick on the other side, and they jumped up and took up their tools and commenced work again on the partition of earth, and in fifteen minutes the middle wall fell out, and they had struck one another to the one-thousandth part of an inch. And there is one everlasting demonstration of the truth of the science of mathematics.

Well, we say that Christianity may be tested just precisely like the science of mathematics may be tested. It is a true science, and you can subject it to the most severe test and demonstrate it for yourself. That is it. Well, here is a man who declares it to be a true science, and says: "I believe in Jesus Christ."

"Well, what makes you believe in Jesus Christ?"

"Because He pardoned my sins."

"Oh, well, there may be a sentiment about that. I do not know about that. None of your foolishness, now. I want to know whether He is divine. I want to know whether He is God or not."

"I will tell you what I will do. Hunt me up a man born blind—one that never saw the light of this world, one whose eyes the doctors have failed to open. Get me a man born stone-blind, that never saw the light of day, and let me see him. Bring him out here. Let us give the world a demonstration that thou art God." Jesus calls the blind man up to Him, and He stoops down and spits on the ground, and makes clay with the spittle. And then he takes the clay and rubs it on the blind man's eyes, and He says, "Now, go and wash in yonder pool."

I expect if some of the scientific of our congregation had been there that day they would have said, "Look at that now, will you? He is making a fool of that poor fellow. Science demonstrates that there are curative properties in dry earth, but wet it, and the curative power is destroyed. To rub inert wet dirt on a man's eyes and tell him to go and wash his eyes in that pool—why, he has washed all over in that pool many a time—there is nothing in it." "Well," the poor, blind fellow says, "Don't you go on speculating. You can afford to speculate on this question, but it is a question of eyesight with me and I am going to try this thing. I heard what He said." And the blind man groped off in the darkness until he struck the edge of the pool and then he stooped and pulled the water up to his eyes and washed the clay from his eyes and then wrung the water out of his eyes, and when he looked up he saw rocks, and rivers and mountains that his eyes had never looked on before. The scientific gentlemen pressed around him, and said, "Look here, old fellow, we want to make something out of this case. We admit he has healed your eyes. We admit all that, but we want you to say he has got a devil."

The poor fellow looked up, with his eyes dancing in his head, and said, "I don't know whether he has a devil or not. I cannot tell you anything about that, but I know, 'whereas I was blind, now I see.'" And, brothers, there is demonstration for you.

"I like that. But can't you demonstrate it some other way?"

"Bring me up ten lepers this way"—and this old world had done its best on lepers in all of its ages, and admitted having done nothing.

They bring those ten lepers up to the Lord Jesus Christ,

and they say: "Master, that we may be made whole." Jesus looked at the poor lepers, and said: "Go and show yourselves to the priest." The poor skeptics yonder say: "Mister, the priests won't let those lepers come around; they will hold up their hands, and tell them to keep off before anybody gets to them."

Oh, how ridiculous they make the poor lepers! Well, the lepers said: "You can argue with the Saviour, but we're going to try this thing; we're going to the priest." Off they start, and before they got one hundred yards from the Son of God, one said: "The scales are falling from my body," and another said: "Such is the case with me," and one said: "I am sound from head to foot," and another said, "I am," and one ran back to praise God for the healing of all.

Do you want a better demonstration of the fact that God Almighty has power and strength to heal a man than when He does such things as these? Put it to the test—that's the question.

I'll tell you what's the matter with this old world. They don't want to test anything.

In this connection, this old world reminds me of a man standing down on the far side of the hill, and I say: "Friend, there is a bright light on the other side of the hill."

He says, "No, there ain't."

I say, "Well, come, I'll show you."

"I ain't going."

I catch him by the hand and I pull him along until I get to the top of the hill, where he can see the light, and as soon as he gets to where he can see the light he turns his head over so he can't see, and I turn his head back so he can see the light, and he shuts his eyes so he can't see, and

I pry his eyes open, and he says, "I don't want to see. It'll cost me something to see that light."

I say to a friend here in this town—he don't believe in railroads, he don't believe a locomotive can run a lick; he has looked at them, he has examined them; they weigh about forty tons, and he doesn't see how they can run—I say to him: "Well, friend, I have ridden on that train. It can run forty miles an hour. It can run from here to Nashville in eleven hours—340 miles."

"Oh, well," he says, "you can't fool me."

"Well," I say, "friend, there is something important in this move. I want to get you on my side, and now come down with me and I will show you."

"Well," he says, "I ain't got the money to spare."

"Well, I will pay your way. What do you say?"

"Well, I ain't going to. I don't believe it. The train don't move at all."

Now, you ain't got time to fool away with that fellow at all—have you?

And here is a grand science proposing to make the best for the universe, and we stand up prepared to prove what it has done, and that man stands up there and says practically on his lips, "I don't believe a word of it."

Now, brother, you may test this thing. And when an infidel sits down and proposes to argue with me, I don't argue with him. I just ask him three questions, and when he gets through answering them the argument is closed, so far as I am concerned.

He says: "I don't believe Jesus Christ has power on earth to forgive sins."

I say: "Have you ever tried Him? Have you ever tried Him?"

"No."

233

"Well, will you try Him?"

"No."

"Well, will you acknowledge you are a fool?"

"No."

"Now, you see, we can't argue this thing any further. That just settles the matter right there."

"I have never tried Him, I am never going to try Him, and I ain't a fool."

Now, when a man denies everything that you want to assert, then there is no ground there for an argument at all, and I just bid him good-by, and we go off, and I feel like I have done right, in that I have not wasted my time on a case like that.

If any man will do his will, he shall know of the doctrine. And when those scribes and Pharisees and hypocrites stood around Christ and were probing and dissecting and analyzing every word He said, Jesus turned around and threw the gauntlet down right at their feet, and said, to put the thing to the test, "And if you don't find it true, I will acknowledge myself an impostor and blasphemer in the sight of God and angels. What more do you want than that?" And I—if you will pardon the expression—I dare any man who doubts—I dare you to give up your sins and take him who is a saviour from sin as your portion.

Now, it is important we stop right at this point and find out what is the will of God concerning a sinner.

Now, what is it? Peter learned at the feet of Jesus Himself what the duty of a sinner was. What did Peter say that day he had 3,000 converts under one sermon? He said: "Repent, ye, therefore, and be converted, that your sins may be blotted out. Repent! repent! repent!"

Now, brother, repentance is your part; salvation from

sin is God's part with the world; and you need never expect God to do His part until you have done your part.

I heard of an old Hardshell once—he was not a converted Hardshell; he was an unconverted Hardshell—and that's the worst shape I have found the devil in yet. He was an unconverted Hardshell, and he would say, "What is to be is to be, you know," and he says, 'If you seek religion you can't find it, and if you find it you ain't got it, and if you've got it you can't lose it, and if you lose it you don't have it." And this is the way the world goes with him. But when you strike an Armenian sinner, a sinner who says, "I must do something; I must seek if I would find. I must knock if I would have the door opened. I must ask if I would receive," he says: "Well, thank God, if I seek religion, I'll find it, and if I find it, I've got it, and if I've got it I can lose it, and if I lose it, I've had it." And he works along on that plan. And, after all, brethren, I want to be the Armenian before I get religion, and a good Hardshell after I get it. Now, that is how I fix the thing. But God Almighty deliver me from Hardshellism before I get it. I am gone, certain. If I get to be a Hardshell before I get to be a Christian I am gone sure.

Now, this old Hardshell was about sixty years old. The preacher said: "We've got a good meeting; I wish you would come down to the meeting and give your heart to God." "Oh," said the Hardshell, "I have been listening for that still, small voice for sixty years." "Have you heard it?" "No." "Well, you're getting pretty deaf, and if you couldn't hear it when your ears were good, how do you expect to hear it now?" He told the old Hardshell: "You come to the meeting and seek God and you will find Him." And, to his astonishment, the old Hardshell was down at the altar and on his knees and praying that night. And next morning, before the service was concluded, the Hardshell was converted to God, and he stood up and slapped his hands together, and he said: "Brethren, I tell you that Methodism has done more for me in twelve hours than Hardshellism did for me in sixty years." He did, sure. And, now, we tell him, "if Methodism did that for you, you stay in it, and don't let the devil break in on you." That's my doctrine. But don't you try that thing on you until you get religion. If we seek Him we'll find Him, if we knock, it will be opened, and my duty is to repent. Repent and be converted. Repent of your sins and be turned around.

Be turned around! I have said before—I repeat it to every man here to-night—there is but one road in the moral universe of God, and that one road goes to both worlds. I can take that street out there in front of this church and I can go to anywhere in the world I want to go. That road out there goes to everywhere—don't it? There is not a spot in America that I can't go to from that road out there. And, friends, every road is one road in the moral sense, and every Christian in this world is in the road to heaven, and every sinner is in the road to hell. The only difference between them at all is—here is heaven at that end of the road, and here is hell at this end, and the Christians are all going that way and the sinners all going this way; and it is not which road you are in, but which direction you are going.

I used to think that a fellow had to go a week's journey, and had to cross the hills and mountains and creeks and rivers and jump gullies and swim rivers; I thought it would take him a solid week to get to the road to heaven, but I found, at last, I had been in the road to hell all my life, and all I had to do to go to heaven was to turn around in the road I was in. As soon as you turn around, you are on the road to heaven as soon as anybody.

Old John Knight, of our Conference—Bishop (turning to Bishop Granberry, who was on the platform), you knew him—a saintly old man he was—was sitting back in the church one night listening to George Smith preach, and George was preaching of repentance, and he was agoing it, and he was speaking of evangelical repentance and legal repentance, splitting hairs a mile long and quartering them, showing which was legal repentance and which was evangelical repentance, and old Uncle John Knight sat back there listening to old Uncle Geoge until he was tired, and old Uncle John stood up and said: "George, won't you stop a minute and let me tell them what repentance is?" And George said, "Yes, Uncle John. I always like to hear you talk." And Uncle John started up the aisle this way, and he said, "I am going to hell; I am going to hell; I am going to hell"; and when he got up to about the end of the aisle, he started right back, and he said, "I am going to heaven; I am going to heaven; I am going to heaven. "Now," said he, "George, tell 'em to turn around; that means repentance; that means conversion; and don't stand there splitting hairs on evangelical and legal repentance."

God have mercy on us and show us that His will is that we be converted. And converted means nothing more than turning around. And when a man turns his back on sin and turns to God he is as much on the road to heaven as any man in the universe. God help us to see that. If you want to go to heaven and are on the road to hell, just right about. If you are on the way to heaven and you want to go to hell, Christian, just right about. We have heaven at one end of the road and hell at the other. God help us, all of us, to turn our backs on sin, and then we have turned our backs on hell and our faces on heaven. And then let us move off. That is the will of God. That is it; that is it.

Oh, how I wish I could get five hundred persons to-night that are on the broad road just to see that all that God asks of them is to turn around. It is yours to turn around and then it is God's to bring the times of refreshness on your soul. That is it.

Now, I turn to another point here. The greatest man whose heart Christ ever touched was St. Paul. When he fell down before God the voice said: "Why persecutest thou me?" and he said: "What wilt thou have me to do?" And the Lord said to him: "Rise, stand upon thy feet."

Brother, the first thing a man ought to do is to get up from a life of sin and take a stand for the right. "I will take a stand." That's it. St. Paul put it afterward in this shape: "I fought a good fight." And when St. Paul said, "I fought a good fight," he said two things in that one sentence with a vengeance. First, "I got over on the good side"; second, "I have fought with all my ransomed powers." First, get over on the good side, and when he is clear over, I want a fellow to get so far over the line that if he wants to fall over the line his head will not fall within ten feet of it. If he falls over, I want him to fall clear over.

A Christian has no right in the devil's territory.

A fellow says: "I go in a barroom because I got business in there." But what business has a Christian got in there? —that's the mystery to me.

"Well, I go in there to collect my rents."

Yes, yes; and I'll risk the barkeeper's chances of heaven before I'll risk yours, you old hypocrite, you! You understand that? The barkeepers and whisky men are not the meanest men in this town. But if you can find me a member of the church that runs a house and rents a place of business for them, I will show you a man that is not only as mean as a barkeeper in every other respect, but adds to it the sin of hypocrisy.

I say, let a man stay on God's territory if he is a Christian, and let him stand there with his weapons drawn, and let him fight for the right.

I saw some time ago where a young lady member of the church went to a ball and danced, and died in the ball-room, and it was said further that after a few minutes the devil came right in and gathered up her soul and started off with it. A few minutes more and St. Peter came along, and he saw that a Christian, a member of the church, had died, and he said: "Where's the soul of the member of the church?"

They said: "The devil has just carried it off."

"Well, how long has it been gone?"

"Oh, just a few minutes; not long."

And St. Peter started off at breakneck speed and said he would overtake that soul and the devil shouldn't have it. It was a Christian soul, he said, and away he ran, and presently he overtook the devil, and said: "Hold! Hold on there! You made a mistake this time!"

"What?" said the devil.

"Why, you've got the soul of that girl, and she's a Christian."

"Well," said the devil, "I didn't know that. I got her over in my territory and I reckon she's mine."

Well, now, you can't afford to run over on the devil's side. Anyhow, you'd better mind how you die over there. I want to get back before I die. St. Paul said: "I have fought a good fight." And by that he meant: "I have come

239

over. I have taken a stand on God's side." And when a man takes his stand on God's side the powers of hell rush upon him, almost before he has time to draw his sword. It is like Bunyan pictures it, when his pilgrim is in the Interpreter's house:

I saw, also, that the Interpreter took him again by the hand and led him into a pleasant place, where was built a stately palace, beautiful to behold, at the sight of which Christian was greatly delighted. He saw, also, upon the top thereof certain persons walking, who were clothed all in gold.

And the Interpreter took him and led him up toward the door of the palace; and, behold, at the door stood a great company of men, as desirous to go in, but durst not. There also sat a man a little distance from the door, at a tableside, with a book and his inkhorn before him, to take the name of him that should enter therein. He saw also that in the doorway stood many men in armor to keep it, being resolved to do the men that would enter what hurt and mischief they could. Now was Christian somewhat in amaze.

At last, when every man started back for fear of the armed men, Christian saw a man of a very stout countenance come up to the man that sat there to write, saying: "Set down my name, sir."

And when he had done this he saw the man draw his sword and put a helmet upon his head and rush toward the door upon the armed men, who laid upon him with deadly force. But the man, not at all discouraged, fell to cutting and hacking most fiercely. So after he had received and given many wounds to those that attempted to keep him out, he cut his way through them all, and pressed forward into the palace, at which there was a pleasant voice heard from those that were within, even of those that walked upon the top of the palace, saying:

"Come in! Come in!
Eternal glory thou shalt win."

So he went in and was clothed with such garments as they.

And so with you, brother. After you have fought the good fight, and steel has clanged against steel, and you have warded off blow after blow, and dealt stroke after stroke upon the enemy, until your worn-out blade drops from your nerveless hand, God shall say to you: "Come up higher. You have fought the good fight, and I have helped you! You have conquered and I will crown you."

And heaven is just the other side of the hardest battle man ever fought in the world.

Take a stand for God and the right!

What is the will of God concerning me? Peter said, "Repent and be converted." God said to Paul, "Arise! Stand on your feet."

Take a stand! Take a stand! I have never yet known a Christian man—a man who wanted to be a Christian—to take a stand that God didn't come to him.

Take a stand! I have never yet known a soul to eschew evil and say, "I take a stand for the right," that God didn't come to him.

Sir, what is the will of God concerning me?

Listen just a moment! It is to give up evil and take a stand for the right. Are you willing to do that? There's something very practical about that, brother. Listen: "If any man will do the will of God, he shall know of the doctrine." That is, know it for himself. And then I would have you notice another fact in the text: "If any man—"

That looks in the face a whole world of human beings and points its finger at each one of you and says: "If you, if you, sir—if you, sir, do what God tells you to do, you shall know of the doctrine, whether it be of God or whether Christ spoke it of himself." That's the text.

And I tell you another thing. I'm never troubled with any doubts when I'm doing the will of God. I'm never

241

troubled with any doubts when I'm doing what God tells me to do, and every doubt I have ever had was when I had refused to do something God told me to do, or else I willingly lent myself to evil influences.

It is considered vulgar now, really vulgar, for a man to get up and preach hell to sinners. . . .

It is not polite to believe that way, and many a little fellow has scratched that out of his creed; but he won't be in hell more than fifteen minutes before he will revise his creed and have nothing in it but hell.

S. J.

12. WHY CONTINUE IN SIN?

IT IS CUSTOMARY FOR A PREACHER TO ANNOUNCE HIS TEXT and then discuss it. We generally read our text and then expound it. But, without any purpose or desire to be singular or odd in this case, I shall first preach the sermon and then read the text, because this text is the answer to the question I want you to spend thirty minutes with me in discussing.

This is a wonderful old book from which we get our text. It goes back to the beginning of all things, and forward to the end of all things. In the first chapter of Genesis I read how the evening and the morning were the first day and the second day, and how at the end of the sixth day the sons of God and the angels shouted over a finished world. One chapter of this book is devoted to my origin, and the thousand chapters which follow warn me of my destiny. God devotes one chapter of this book, one page of the book, to telling me whence I come and all the other warnings and all the other rebukes and promises and precepts of His word are but so many index fingers pointing into the great hereafter, warning me of my destiny.

I believe there is but one thing condemned in this book, and that is sin; and sin is the only thing in the universe of God that can permanently harm a soul. Disappointments may sadden me. Vexation and cares may worry me, and the thousand of the environments of earth may fret me. But there is but one thing that can permanently damage the soul, and that is sin. And, really, I don't need any enlightenment from this book or the pulpit to teach me that sin will do its most work on character, on the soul, on my present, on my future destiny. And if it is sin that all the cannon of heaven are turned loose upon; if it is sin that God would not have us commit; if it is sin that heaven frowns upon, and that perdition itself would have us commit; if it is sin—then I stop and ask this question: Why will you continue in sin?

Now we notice a moment the words of this question. They are very simple, and yet they are very forcible: Why will you continue in sin?

Salvation is a personal matter. Damnation is a personal matter. I can get no one to die for me; no one to be buried in my stead; no one to stand before God in my place; no one to pass into glory in my stead; no one to be damned in my place. Salvation is pre-eminently a personal matter. I am saved, if saved at all, thank God—I am saved in myself and for myself. If I am lost, it is me lost, and if every other man should make his way to God, I am shut up to the consciousness that heaven's door is closed in my face, and that I personally am shut up in hell forever. Men sin in groups and go in schools and run with the multitude, but judgment is personal. Salvation is personal. You and I, if we walk into glory, will walk in just as personally and as really as if we were the only ones that left this earth for a better world. If we are damned, we shall be damned as personally as if we were the only men that the sentence of God should rest upon through all eternity. And this question means something.

Why will you?—not why will the church; not why will the preachers; not why will the cities; not why will States; but why will you, you, you? I don't mean the man in front of you, or the one behind you, or the one to your right, or your left. I mean you! you! Why will you continue in sin? Why will you lead this life and continue doing and saying those things and neglecting these things? Why will you?

Now we answer first for you: Is it because you are ignorant of what sin is? Can any man in this house say, "I don't know that it is wrong to swear, and wrong to drink, and wrong to lie, and wrong to rebel, and wrong to live in darkness," when light is proffered? Can any man say that? Can any man raised in the land of Bibles look God and angels in the face and say, "The reason I live here an impenitent sinner is because I don't know what sin is"? Will you say that? Have you never read in that book, "Thou shalt not take the name of the Lord thy God in vain"? Have you never read in that book, "Thou shalt not bear false witness"? Have you never read, "Remember the Sabbath day to keep it holy"? Have you never read, "He that breaketh the least commandment is guilty of all"? Then I ask you, friend, can you say now, or ever, that the reason you leave here impenitent to-night is because you don't know what sin is? Will you say that?

Do you know that every sinner in this land stands self-convicted on that proposition? There's not a sinner in this city that hasn't for years been criticizing the life of the church, and you know that every criticism of your lips on the life of a member of the church is incontestable proof that you know what right is, and that you know what wrong is. You won't suffer these members of the church to do wrong, and when they do do wrong you speak of it, and point the finger of scorn at them.

I know it looks worse for a member of the church to do wrong, and I'll tell you why. The difference between a member of the church and that sinner out of the church is this: that member of the church is like a white piece of canvas, and you sprinkle any kind of mud or dirt on a white piece of canvas and it shows very plainly; and that's the difference between a member of the church and an old sinner out of it.

If I were to go down to-night and get drunk, or if I were to get drunk to-morrow, the telegraph wires of the country would catch it up, and it would be telegraphed all over the face of the Union. "Mr. Jones is drunk."

But there's many an old, red-nosed fellow in this town gets drunk every day and nobody pays any more attention to it than they do to the sun shining. You see, that's the difference between a gentleman and a vagabond!

If I were to step out on the streets to-morrow and swear and profane the name of God, the newspapers would catch it up and declare that I was blaspheming on the streets of this city. But there are ten thousand black-mouthed swearers in this town who profane the name of God every day upon the streets, and people pay no attention whatever to them. Now, you see, that's just the difference between a gentleman and a vagabond!

I'm glad this world makes distinctions. I'm glad. There's some of you won't walk down street but some vagabond will say to you, "Come in and take a drink with me." But I can walk these streets ten years and nobody will ever ask me to take a drink.

This world knows who's who. I'm so glad this world will let a gentleman pass on and let him alone. I'm glad of that.

Well, then, I ask you again, is it because you are ignorant

of the consequences of sin? Will you say that? Is there a man here who never read in that book, "The wicked shall be turned into hell"?

But you say, "Forsooth, and there is no hell." I know the cry of this nineteenth century is, "There is no hell," and I am sorry to see that in all this land, where men have sworn eternal allegiance to that book, there is not one preacher in twenty to-day that will stand up and preach hell as that book asserts it.

Why is it considered vulgar now, really vulgar, for a man to get up and preach hell to sinners? Don't you know that it is so? And I want to say to you this: I will take the records of the Church of God and every preacher that had power with God and influence with men, and that brought thousands to Christ, every one of them—I run back, and I will take Bunyan, and I will take Whitefield, and I will take Jonathan Edwards, and I will take Charles G. Finney, and I will take your own leading evangelist in America, Dwight L. Moody. I will take C. H. Spurgeon, in London, and every man that had power with God and influence with men—believed in a real, genuine, Scriptural brimstone hell! Now, what do you say?

It is not polite to believe that way and many a little fellow has scratched that out of his creed; but he won't be in hell more than fifteen minutes before he will revise his creed, and have nothing in it but hell. I am sorry for a fellow fooling away his time that way. And I want to say to you to-night, the biggest fool this world ever saw is the man that gets in the biggest, broadest, plainest road to hell, and stops on the way trying to persuade people there is no such place as hell! The biggest fool this world ever looked on is the man that spends all his probationary existence trying to persuade himself that there is no hell, and then, after death, he lays down in hell, forever realizing that there is one.

You say, "Well, I don't like these hell-scared sinners." Why, bless you, they are the only sort I do like. And I want to tell you to-night, fourteen years ago I got a good scare, and, blessed be God! I ain't got over it good yet, and I never want to get over it until I get into the pearly gates, safe forever. And I believe in a hell just as strong as I believe in heaven, and I believe that a topless heaven has its counterpart in a bottomless hell. And just in proportion as you let up at this point, that minute you run riot in wickedness and sin and outrageous conduct; and I want to say to you all to-night, my fellow citizens, I believe that if a man lives and dies in his sins, because that book says so, that he is lost—and lost forever! If heaven is eternal, then hell is eternal, for the same adjectives that apply to one apply to the other; and this much I say, "God help me, God help me, that I may never go there!"

A man asked me the other day where hell was? Said I: "I don't know, and by the grace of God I never will know—I never will know." And he asked me was there really, genuine, burning brimstone there? Said I: "I am so afraid there is, that I am never going there, and I am never going to see whether there is or not." God keep the gate of heaven wide open before me, and some of these days I will run right into glory and to God; and then, in heaven, shut up forever, I shall be delivered from hell forever.

No, sir, no man here can say, "The reason I live here a sinner is because I don't know what sin will lead to." I like very well the definition of the old colored woman. When the old man came home he said, "Auntie, the preacher preached to-day about hell fire and brimstone," and he said,

"Auntie, where does God get all the brimstone to burn forever?" The old woman said, "Honey, all the old sinners takes the brimstone with 'em there to burn 'em forever."

Then I come closer to you with this question. You say you will leave here a sinner to-night—and men will do it to-night. Impenitent sinners, you will leave here that way. Well, why? It is not because you are ignorant of the nature of sin, and ignorant of its consequences. You know what sin is, and you know what sin will do for a man, and I know that sin will ruin a man in this world, and I know that sin is the same in all worlds. Men are the same in all worlds, and it is not a question how long man will endure, but how long will sin endure.

Then, I ask you again, is it because you are indifferent to the truth? You know what the truth is, and you know what sin will do for you, and yet you are indifferent to the truth. Oh, how many indifferent men in this world wear a placid countenance when every nerve and muscle in them ought to be shaking under the pressure and power of truth as it is applied to them! Oh, how many indifferent men here to-night—indifferent to the truth, indifferent to their condition—and may be in twenty-four hours from this moment they will be in eternity and their body in their coffin; and yet they are perfectly indifferent to the future—indifferent! And I do thank God that whatever may have been my estate as a sinner, thank God, I never reached the point when I was indifferent to the truth. Sometimes I would not go to church once in six months, with the bells ringing all around me Sabbath morning, and yet I say to you to-night, I never went with my Christian wife to the house of God and heard an honest gospel sermon that it didn't move me from head to foot. I tried to appear indifferent. I would not let my wife know how I felt for all the world; I would not let the preacher know it for all the world; and yet I carried a placid, indifferent countenance through it all. And yet that man out there says to-night: "That is my condition, I feel a good deal different from what my wife thinks anything about and what my neighbor thinks anything about; I am concerned about the great hereafter." It is not indifference.

Then I ask you, Is it because you are reckless as to the consequences? Sometimes men put on an air of recklessness and sometimes they seem to defy God and defy man. They curse with a loud voice and sin with an outstretched arm, and they think, "I have nothing to conceal; I sin publicly and openly; I defy God to His face," and there is a recklessness that is enough to make men tremble as they look upon it. Recklessness! You say, "How foolish these things!"

In my own town one night, one of our citizens, a daring, reckless, drinking man, stood on the platform of the depot, and he said: "To-night I am going to walk up the railroad and meet the down passenger night express, and," said he, "I am going to meet it on the track and gather the engine in my hands and hurl it into the ditch on the side of the track." They laughed at him, felt his recklessness had assumed a very humorous turn, and that night as the down passenger train came rolling and thundering down, just a quarter above the depot, this maddened, reckless wretch met it on the track and stooped to catch it by its fender, and it rushed and rolled on and he was ground to powder. Oh, how reckless that man was! And there is that man rushing right up into the face of God and His judgment, and by and by, instead of tossing God and judgment to one side, "upon whom this stone shall fall, it shall grind him to powder."

You say: "I am not a reckless man." There's many a man

appears to be reckless, but when he turns off the gas at night and sits alone with God he is afraid of God, and he is afraid of the judgment, and he is afraid of eternity, and he is afraid of the great beyond. "No, sir, it is not recklessness," you say. "It is not because I am satisfied with my present condition." Then I ask you again: "Is it because you are leading a sort of a compromise life—'I am going to be religious after a while'?" If I were to make this proposition this moment—if I ask every man in this house who intends to prepare for death between this and his dying moment, to rise, every one in this house would stand up immediately. No man ever settled and fixed the question unalterably and forever, "I have made up my mind to be damned." I never saw the man that would say that. Then, brother, have you and I any more time to throw away? I have often thought of that little fellow running down to the train with all his might, and just as he reached the depot the train rolled off, and there he stood, sad and disappointed and dejected, and a kind friend looked on the little fellow and said, "My little man, I will tell you what is the matter." "What?" said the boy. "Oh," said the man, "you didn't run fast enough." "Oh, yes, I did," said the boy, "I ran with all my might, but my trouble was I didn't start soon enough." And, oh, me! there's many a man in this world that will miss heaven, not because he didn't start, but because he didn't start soon enough. And I have seen the passenger stand at the depot platform and the train had gone, had gone, had gone, and I looked into his face and I saw written upon every tissue and ligament of his countenance, "Left! Left! Left!" And when the last hope shall have swept by you and gone on without you, then upon every fiber and tissue of your soul will be written, "Left and lost! Lost and left forever."

Oh, my Lord, teach men that while God Almighty runs His trains right at our feet every day, and checks up enough for us all to get aboard, it is the bounden duty of every man to step on board and go to God and to glory.

A great many people think, "Well, I'm going to quit doing wrong; I have made up my mind for that." Yes. What is that worth? Here is a man whose all depends on his reaching Cincinnati to-morrow morning at 8 o'clock. He goes down there to the depot to-night and stands there and lets the trains all pull out and leave him. You will say, "Friend, you have lost your all." "I know that." "Well, why didn't you get on board?" "Well, I—I—I came down here to the train, and I—I—I thought if I wouldn't throw any rocks at the engineer and I wouldn't cuss the conductor, the thing would take me along anyhow. I thought all that was necessary was for me not to bother the engineer and conductor." And there's many a man in this world standing and being left forever who expects to get in at last because he didn't cuss the preacher and throw rocks at the meetinghouse. There's a good deal of that sort of foolishness in this world.

Then we come at you with this question: You say, "No, sir, I will not lead a compromise life. I know I ought to be religious, but I have not set a day ahead." Then I ask you this question: "Is it because a spiritual apathy has taken possession of your soul?"

Listen, brother:

> Awake thou that sleepest, and arise from the dead, and Christ shall give thee light.

The saddest attitude of the soul as it lies on the brink of perdition is the attitude of slumber. A man sleeping over his immortal interests! Can you imagine a man like that? I have seen the soul of a man just in that condition. I have worked with him, prayed with him and wrestled with him day after day and week after week, and the devil would administer opiates to his soul and he would say: "Just let me sleep until this service is over—this last hour's service of the meeting. Just let me sleep through this." And I have aroused him and we have sung, "Come, humble sinner," and on and on, and then he said: "Just let me sleep through this last verse."

> But if I die, that mercy sought,
> That on the King have cried,
> It's then to die—delightful thought—
> As sinner never died.

And he sang the verse through, and he closed his eyes and slept and slept and slept, until in hell he opened his eyes, wide awake forever! Oh, brother, can you sleep that way? Oh, brother! How men sleep over the interest of their souls!

I can arouse this town with the cry that there is danger to a family here. In the city of Atlanta, a few months ago, the Wilson House, one of our second-class hotels—in size, I mean—caught fire. The flames burst out of the window, and directly the fire bells commenced ringing, the fire companies came thundering down the street, and multitudes pressed toward the hotel. The servants ran from room to room and awakened the guests. They waked up this one and he dressed hurriedly and ran out. They waked up that one and he dressed hurriedly and ran out.

Finally, a servant went to one room in which there were two guests, each in a different bed. He aroused one. He jumped out of bed. He aroused the other, but with a moan and a groan he went to sleep again. The guest who had been aroused dressed himself hurriedly and ran to the bed

255

of the other and shook him and said, "Get up, the house is on fire." The man simply moaned and groaned and went back to sleep. When his friend had finished dressing, he ran to the bed and pulled the man out of bed. He stood him on his feet and said, "The house is on fire! Hurry, hurry, or you will be burned up!" The man as he was turned loose shot back into his bed with a moan and a groan, and went to sleep again. And the next day, when they were raking among the debris of the building, they found his bones all charred and burned. And many a time on earth, heaven seems to long to arouse us and pull us away from our surroundings and stand us on our feet and cry, "Fire! Eternal fire!" and yet there we stand, and at last among sulphurous flames and eternal perdition, our bones lie burned and charred forever.

Look here, friends, if we wake to-night, let us stand up like men and flee from the wrath to come.